NEITHER DEVIL NOR CHILD

NEITHER DEVIL NOR CHILD

HOW WESTERN ATTITUDES ARE HARMING AFRICA

TOM YOUNG

ONEWORLD

A Oneworld Book

First published by Oneworld Publications, 2018

Copyright © Tom Young 2018

The moral right of Tom Young to be identified as the
Author of this work has been asserted by him in accordance
with the Copyright, Designs, and Patents Act 1988

ISBN 978-1-78607-063-0
eISBN 978-1-78607-064-7

Typeset by Palimpsest Book Production Limited, Falkirk, Stirlingshire
Printed and bound in Great Britain by Clays Ltd, St Ives plc

Oneworld Publications
10 Bloomsbury Street
London WC1B 3SR
England

Stay up to date with the latest books,
special offers, and exclusive content from
Oneworld with our monthly newsletter

Sign up on our website
oneworld-publications.com

CONTENTS

PREFACE

In the late 1990s, Mozambique was required by the International Monetary Fund (IMF) and the World Bank to privatise its state-owned banks. The process was notoriously corrupt and attracted attention because a well-known Mozambican journalist who was investigating it, as well as the head of the central bank's supervision unit, were both murdered in mysterious circumstances. Shortly after these events, donors approved a debt-reduction scheme for the country. Since then, Mozambique has continued to receive very high volumes of foreign aid and to be held up as a success story. The World Bank representative in the capital city of Maputo said, 'Without a doubt, Mozambique is a success story, a success both in terms of growth but also as a model for other countries as to how to get the best possible out of donor interest.' Then British Secretary of State for International Development, Hilary Benn, averred that, 'Mozambique sets an example across Africa and the Developing World.' Not to be outdone, the IMF gave its 2014 Africa conference in Maputo the title 'Africa Rising: Building to the Future'.

Despite these confident assertions, the fact is that Mozambique continues to be desperately poor, ranked 180th out of 188 states in 2014, and by the end of 2015 had not achieved any of the Millennium Development Goals. But a small section of the population, especially those connected to the ruling party, Frelimo, have done extraordinarily well. Its one-time president, Armando Guebuza, dubbed 'Mr Guebusiness', is probably the richest man in the country. Shortly after he stood down, Mozambique was forced to approach the IMF for emergency financial support, as it became clear that the government had secretly contracted more than $2 billion in new debt, breaching its agreements with donors as well as its own domestic laws. A considerable amount of this money is still unaccounted for.

The gap between rhetoric and reality could not be wider, and such situations often provoke angry reactions. But we need to look harder and ask how we got here. In pursuit of that I have started from two intuitions. The first is that ideas are important in politics. Such a view is widely derided on grounds of common sense both by those engaged in politics and those who study it. Politics, it is said, is all about the calculation of interests, hard-headedness, ruthlessness and pragmatism. (As an American president once asserted, 'It's the economy, stupid.') Doubting this does not mean we must subscribe to a wishy-washy idealism or the illusion that everybody is, or can be, selfless. But it does imply that there is much to be learnt from studying how attitudes and action are informed by ideas. The second intuition concerns the extraordinary range of activities that various agencies have pursued in Africa since independence. These agencies do much more than instruct African states to sell banks or not borrow money: they overthrow governments, they finance military forces, they provide large amounts of foreign aid, they try to change people's values and practices, they even tell people what school textbooks to use. My second intuition is that all these activities, though they vary over time and are shared across many different kinds of bodies, are linked, and are part of a common effort that, for want of a better term, I call the Western Project.

A central argument of this book is that this project has a history. In 1898, Rudyard Kipling published a poem, 'The White Man's Burden', which, although it was intended to support the US invasion of the Philippines, provided a praise poem for imperial rule more generally. It calls on the white man to rule, for their own good, 'your new-caught, sullen peoples, / Half-devil and half-child'. This poem is, of course, regarded today as the very pinnacle of racist awfulness; but stripped of its overtly racial language it voices assumptions and aspirations that have by no means disappeared – though this suggestion would be hotly rejected by many of those involved in the Western Project.

These are controversial matters which prompt one final comment on my approach. The study of human affairs cannot produce the kinds of truth that are possible in mathematics, science or medicine. This does not mean that 'anything goes', because we must make our best efforts to consider evidence and argument in good faith. But it does mean that, having done those things, there are no areas of human activity and enquiry where there do not remain fundamental differences of under-standing or belief. So in this book I have not hesitated to explain certain concepts ('civil society', 'democracy', 'human rights') and to indicate where my arguments differ from those of others. Likewise, in the reading guide at the end of the book, I have indicated a variety of writings that show the range of disagree-ment about certain issues, as well as the writings that have shaped my own view. In human affairs we simply have to acknowledge that the boundary between explanation and advo-cacy is flexible. So the broader purpose of this book goes beyond explanation to argue that Kipling was indeed wrong, but so also are many of those currently engaged in foisting on Africa a project that is in many ways misconceived, and should be aban-doned.

1

GUILT

THERE IS A STORY THAT THE West tells about Africa. It has been ethically persuasive, psychologically and politically powerful. Like all good stories it comes in different versions and appeals to different audiences. It can be made more or less complex and it links emotionally charged themes and images to wider ideas and agendas. Also, like all good stories, it contains elements of truth. But unlike a novel or a play, it is not simply a work of imagination. Social and political stories, the kinds of stories we tell to make sense of our interaction with others, are rarely based on fabrication; they are about selection and presentation and plausibility. So, unlike fiction, social and political stories have many authors. The mainstream Africa story has been produced by writers (academics, journalists, activists) and organisations (policy institutes, governments, international organisations). It has been popularised and publicised by politicians, lobby groups, political movements, even entertainers. It has found its way into university and school curricula, images, memorials, ceremonies and indeed fiction. All of those involved in producing it have seen themselves as presenting a truth. So the mainstream Africa story is not in any simple sense 'false', nor is it a 'myth', and for that reason it cannot be 'refuted'. But that story does contain omissions and distortions, and unless they are challenged by other stories, they will have damaging consequences. The three main elements that make up this story are colonialism, race and slavery. These are, of course, very large topics, and my concern here is not with explaining their historical development but with clarifying the orthodoxy. The aim is to make sense of what they say, and what they leave out or gloss over, and to see how that fits into the overarching story or narrative. It will then be possible to understand the political effects of the story.

COLONIALISM

Colonialism is the most important element in the story for two main reasons. The first is that the colonial conquest of Africa was achieved, unlike most other parts of the world, remarkably quickly and completely. The second is that this conquest was justified by the idea of a 'civilising mission'. Around 1800, European powers possessed little more than footholds in Africa and were almost entirely ignorant of the interior. Between about 1880 and 1910 there was a 'scramble for Africa' which brought the whole continent, with the exceptions of Liberia and Ethiopia, under European rule. Britain and France took the lion's share, but Portugal, Belgium and Germany all occupied considerable territories, while even Spain and Italy had a share. Remarkably, during this process, the colonial powers agreed to avoid conflict over these territories and publicly justified their occupation partly on the grounds that they were abolishing slavery and bringing progress to a 'backward' region. Powerful states have often used lofty claims to dress up self-interested actions, but at the time, and indeed for some time afterwards, colonialism was seen as a noble endeavour. Many of the most prominent critics of colonial rule in the nineteenth century, those who had for example helped to bring to an end the Belgian King Leopold's vicious regime in the Congo, were not against colonialism in principle but rather the deficiencies in its practice. Even many on the political left shared these views. Karl Marx, never one to pass up a chance to denounce the brutality of British colonial rule in India, nonetheless saw it as historically 'progressive', and likely to bring about positive change in the long term. His comrade-in-arms, Friedrich Engels, said much the same about the French annexation of Algeria and even the American annexation of northern Mexico.* Many others, while they shared misgivings about the brutality and destructiveness of colonial conquest, reluctantly conceded that a complete absence of rule might leave populations vulnerable to abuse and exploitation by private interests, as had already occurred in the Congo. Until well after 'the scramble', almost no one in Europe was against colonial rule in Africa.

Barely a hundred years later, colonialism is an unspeakable crime. The idea of colonialism as 'progressive', much less the assumption of even partially benign motives, has become not merely unthinkable, but derisory, indeed part of the history of colonial oppression itself. How can we account for such a dramatic turnaround? First, the pace of progress in the colonial territories, even by the rather modest standards promised, was extremely slow. The British government started talking about 'development' (in its modern sense) in the 1920s, but the resources devoted to it were extremely limited. Claims that colonial rule was essentially benign or progressive came to ring increasingly hollow. More importantly, the Second World War had required both massive military and ideological mobilisation

---

* Marx and Engels later shifted their ground on these issues, but outright objection in principle remained very rare.

against a Nazi enemy, an enemy which had explicitly proclaimed an ideology of group domination. Even during the war, the Allies had begun to express their war aims in terms of human equality, terms which were incompatible with alien rule over whole peoples. After the war, as the horrors of the Third Reich became more widely known, any sort of view which condoned, even temporarily, such rule, became irredeemably discredited. The very self-confidence that made colonialism possible was already collapsing, even if colonial rule itself staggered on for a few more years. As institutions and practices became more and more suspect, the testimony of colonisers became ever more dubious until it came to seem self-evidently false. If the colonisers said they encountered widespread tribal warfare, they must have been lying, perhaps even engineering such warfare in order to legitimate their rule. If the colonisers reported widespread slavery in Africa which they were concerned to abolish, that was the fault of colonialism (and the slave trade). If the colonisers said they aimed to improve the physical condition of African populations, they were only doing so in order to mislead humanitarian opinion back home, or insofar as conditions did improve, it was only intended to further the exploitation of Africans.

It is not difficult to paint a very grim picture of the colonial period. Colonial conquest was often brutal, made more so by the rapid development of new kinds of firearms in the late nineteenth century, such as rapid-firing weapons and mobile artillery, which opened up a huge technological gap between European armies and others that no amount of courage could compensate for. At the Battle of Omdurman in 1898, British forces killed some 10,000 Sudanese fighters for the loss of some 50 of their own. At its very worst, colonial rule was little more than a reign of terror, as for example in Leopold's Congo. The German massacre of the Herero in South West Africa in 1904 resulted in thousands of deaths due to lack of food and water.

Less well known, and on a smaller scale, are the depredations of more or less psychopathic individuals pursuing their own sometimes demented agendas. Aside from such premeditated violence, colonial conquest had many unforeseen consequences, such as the spread of disease and the disruption of traditional forms of husbandry. In colonies where there was white settlement, Africans were driven off their land. Colonial states did not hesitate to resort to forced labour for public works projects, such as railway construction, where fatality rates were often very high. Some colonial powers coerced African labour into working for settlers, or imposed forced cultivation of certain crops.

All these points add up to an indictment so powerful that for many they make further comment superfluous. But, however compelling we find this evidence, everything we know about eighteenth- and nineteenth-century Africa suggests it was already an extremely violent place. Incongruous as it may seem, large-scale inter-African violence was effectively brought to an end by colonial rule. Colonial authorities did, from time to time, turn a blind eye to low-level raiding in marginal areas, but the one thing they did do was enforce peace. Of course, they had their own reasons for doing so, but the imposition of peace had beneficial side effects. First was the simple fact of increased personal security. Population statistics provide evidence for this. Although colonial rule had often been brutally imposed and was sometimes extremely costly in terms of African life, once it was consolidated African populations grew quite quickly, even in the Belgian Congo. Another side effect was that enforced peace made possible greatly increased mobility – not just of people, but of goods. Markets could now function more effectively, and areas of food shortage could now be more easily supplied. There is some truth in the argument that colonial states tried to prevent Africans exploiting economic opportunities, but it is often overstated. The fact is that, under colonial rule, new technologies became available, towns expanded, movement became easier and more secure, and economic opportunities, both for work and trade, were widened. It has been argued that such developments served only to enhance colonial rule, and exploit colonial economies. That is of course true, but how could it be otherwise? All states seek ways to utilise resources and generate revenue. In that sense, independent African states have been no different from colonial ones. The real issue was the division of the rewards, and while it is certainly true that colonial rulers skewed the benefits towards the colonial state and Europeans more generally, they could not, and in many cases did not wish to, entirely exclude Africans. A road can be used by anyone, as can a safe market or a currency.

Africans often seized the new opportunities available to them. The explosion of cocoa production in the Gold Coast or the development of plantation agriculture in Côte d'Ivoire between the wars was not engineered by Europeans or colonial states but by African farmers responding to demand. In 1900 virtually no cocoa was produced in Gold Coast. Thirty years later, total production reached 250,000 tonnes, and the Gold Coast was the world's largest exporter. In time, colonial states came to see the value of this economic activity and sought to encourage it because it produced tax revenue.

Colonialism brought with it a great deal of cultural baggage as well and, no less than material technologies, the effects of this were mixed. But Africans could not be wholly excluded from exploring opportunities in this sphere either. Colonial rule was also literate rule. Out of necessity colonial states needed literate African employees, initially as clerks and translators, later as teachers or lower level officials. In the more prosperous colonies, such as Nigeria and the Gold Coast, there was a fairly rapid growth in the number of Africans with professional skills such as medicine and law. An increasingly literate African population began to exploit the possibilities of literacy in all sorts of ways: the creation of an African press led to the cultivation of 'public opinion', both of which led inevitably to debate on social and political matters. Much of that reflection and debate turned to new ideas that came with colonial rule, notably the idea of 'the state' as a unified, territorial entity to which all citizens owed allegiance. It was these ideas, among other things, that encouraged the beginnings of African nationalism and demands for independence.

If the mainstream account of colonialism as *nothing but* a system of oppression and exploitation is misleading, in what other ways does it obscure some of the truth? For all its championing of Africans, it does so in ways which actually marginalise them. The mainstream story attributes implausible degrees of malevolence and power to the colonialists while attributing similarly implausible degrees of benevolence and powerlessness to African peoples. The history of colonialism becomes a morality play, little more than an endless saga in which evil white men do unspeakable things to good black men and women. This is not to treat Africans as equals at all but to treat them as somehow unsullied, and it flies in the face of historical evidence. Much of that evidence suggest that Africans, or certainly their rulers, were just as ready to engage in the violent conquest, destruction or absorption of other groups and cultures as any other society. These tendencies were so pronounced that some historians talk about an 'African scramble for Africa'. And there is plentiful historical evidence to suggest that African rulers were eager to pursue projects of conquest in alliance with Europeans, where they might gain an advantage. The Ethiopian monarchy in the nineteenth century was imperialist, annexing territory to the south of its heartlands. Usman dan Fodio founded the Sokoto caliphate (in what is now northern Nigeria and Niger) through active conquest and made it probably the largest state in nineteenth-century Africa. Samori Ture was perhaps the most famous of the West African empire builders, feted now as a hero of African nationalism, but whose war-making involved constant raiding, military conscription, enslavement and forced religious conversion, so much so that it sparked resistance by other African societies that made the eventual French conquest of what are now Guinea and Mali much easier. Indeed, even after European military and political domination became overwhelming, tacit arrangements could still be mutually beneficial and did continue under colonial rule. For instance, the Mourides (Islamic Brotherhoods) of Senegal collaborated closely with the French colonial authorities and instructed their followers not only to accept colonial rule but also forced labour and military conscription.

So the mainstream story obscures historical realities which show the similarities of many kinds of conquest, as well as excluding the complex political calculations that entered into the various forms of colonial rule. The hard truth is that, almost everywhere, colonial rule was a collaborative enterprise. Colonial states could usually bring decisive force to bear in emergencies, but Africans were not prostrate before some all-powerful colonial leviathan. Aside from anything else, colonial states were desperately short of workers. Vast territories were managed by very small groups of officials, whose primary responsibility was to keep the peace and, if possible, to collect taxes with the absolute minimum of force. While overwhelming force could be mobilised, its use carried severe political costs back home where it was not popular with metropolitan governments or public opinion. So, in practice, maintaining peace and collecting usually modest taxes required some degree of cooperation and compromise.

RACE

Everywhere in the nineteenth and early twentieth centuries, European powers annexed huge territories. Even where annexation proved impossible (China, Turkey, Persia, Siam) such territories were often reduced to a subordinate status, under the 'influence' of one or more of the major European powers. So what makes Africa so different? Why should colonialism form such an important part of the mainstream story about Africa? We do not have to look far for clues. In public discourse, colonialism is associated with one of the most emotionally charged issues of our times: race. What makes colonialism in Africa so incendiary, so different from everywhere else, so potent a weapon of denunciation even now, is that it seems to be not only about economic exploitation but also a form of specifically racial oppression. Colonialism can be seen as one of a whole cluster of practices that denigrate black people. There has been widespread cultural contempt for, and hostility towards, Africans throughout Western culture. Indeed, some of the greatest European thinkers espoused views that are, by today's standards, offensive and 'racist'.* The great Scottish philosopher David Hume once wrote:

> I am apt to suspect the negroes and in general all other species of men (for there are four or five different kinds) to be naturally inferior to the whites. There never was a civilized nation of any other complexion than white, nor even any individual eminent either in action or speculation. No ingenious manufactures amongst them, no arts, no sciences… [T]here are NEGROE slaves dispersed all over EUROPE, of which none ever discovered any symptoms of ingenuity; tho' low people, without education, will start up amongst us, and distinguish themselves in every profession. In JAMAICA, indeed, they talk of one negroe as a man of parts and learning; but 'tis likely he is admired for very slender accomplishments, like a parrot, who speaks a few words plainly.

---

* I place this word in quotation marks here to suggest that the term has become extremely imprecise.

The German philosopher Hegel asserted, in his *Philosophy of History*, that 'Africa proper, as far as history goes back, has remained – for all purposes of connection with the rest of the world – shut up; it is the Gold-land compressed within itself – the land of childhood, which lying beyond the day of self-conscious history, is enveloped in the dark mantle of night'. Even Charles Darwin, whose lifelong hostility to slavery is common knowledge, stands accused of racism in his great work, *On the Origin of Species by Means of Natural Selection, or the Preservation of Favoured Races in the Struggle for Life*, and various remarks in his *Descent of Man* suggest that 'the civilised races of man will almost certainly exterminate, and replace, the savage races throughout the world'. The suggestion that such quotations are indicative of a deep-seated racism is often made in the strongest possible form, dismissing the idea that such thinkers merely shared the common prejudices of their age, and asserting rather that racial thinking was an integral part of their understanding of the world, that they were not only complicit in, but also actively helped to legitimate, racial oppression. In the middle to late nineteenth century, attitudes did harden and judgements about African peoples became harsher. Much of this was shaped by the apparently huge disparity between the technological accomplishments of European and African societies which, combined with a kind of lazy evolutionism, suggested to many contemporaries that such social differences were deep-seated, possibly ineradicable. Colonial practice tended to follow these attitudes and all the colonial empires practised forms of racial distancing, whether they acknowledged it or not.

So at first blush, an overwhelming body of evidence allows us to say that racism has long been a pervasive part of Western culture, inflicting physical and psychological damage on Africans. What else can there be to say? I would add a caution that people are reluctant to question the words they use, particularly if they carry a powerful critical charge – think of words like 'fascism',

'oppression', 'pro-choice'. These are words that have become politically powerful, and their function is psychological: they work
to identify an enemy and to mobilise energies. So what questions
should we ask about 'race' and 'racism'? Both words are highly
ambiguous, not least because they occupy that rather tricky area
between biological and social science. It seems impossible, in
the light of modern scientific knowledge, to imagine that there
are different races in any fundamental, genetic sense. But there
are what biology calls phenotypical differences (skin colour, hair
texture and so on) which people use as classifiers in everyday
social interaction, and in modern times are used by states in
pursuit of policies like affirmative action. These usages slide into
what social science calls 'ethnic' differences, that is to say notions
of culture, including beliefs and practices and so on. While such
distinctions may not be useful for biologists, they have shaped
our social reality. Much the same difficulties and ambiguities
recur when we question 'racism'. At its most vague, 'racism' can
mean virtually any kind of negative value judgement about the
physical features, cultural practices or beliefs of a human group;
at its most precise it combines the notion of racial hierarchy of
superior and inferior groups, combined with an urge on the
part of supposedly superior groups to exclude or dominate
supposedly inferior groups.

Such considerations should give us pause for thought in the
face of strident accusations that whole societies or whole theo-
ries are plainly and simply 'racist'. To return to the writers
discussed above, the accusations of racism rely on a tiny proportion of texts, presented without context or explanation on the
assumption that they are self-evident indictments. The dispute
about Hume turns on one footnote, some few lines of text, which
appeared in one version, not all, of one essay. If racism is such
an integral part of Hume's thought, why is there so little of it?
One can of course always play the quotation game the other
way and quote Hegel to the effect that 'man is implicitly rational;

herein lies the possibility of equal justice for all men and the futility of a rigid distinction between races which have rights and those which have none', or that 'Reason must maintain that the slavery of the Negroes is a wholly unjust institution, one which contradicts true justice, both human and divine, and which is to be rejected.' Sometimes these selective quotes are based on simple misunderstandings: in the title of Darwin's famous work, the term 'races' does not yet hold its modern connotations (there is virtually nothing about human beings in the *Origin of Species*).

Accusations often fail to distinguish between the personal leanings of thinkers and the structure and implications of their thinking. Similarly they often fail to distinguish a thinker from the effects of their thought. The writings of Marx and Engels are full of contemptuous remarks about all sorts of people, especially Slavs. But nowhere in history have people who really were racists turned to Marx and Engels for inspiration, and many who struggled against racial oppression found that Marxism helped them to fashion arguments and strategies against such oppression. The fact is that using selective quotation, you could make virtually anyone writing before about 1970 sound like a 'racist'.

It is hard to build any consistent picture of unrelieved 'racism' in Western thought, given the huge variation in attitudes. The word 'race' is rarely used with any consistency, certainly not in the nineteenth or the early twentieth century. There was no consensus as to its exact meaning and it could be used as a synonym for 'nation', 'people' or 'ethnic group'. Both Christianity and Liberalism, whatever historical compromises they have made at times, provide insuperable obstacles to taking race seriously as a form of social and political organisation. So while it is fair to say that certain historical periods have aligned race with perceived 'backwardness' to justify racial arrogance, particularly towards those with darker skin, virtually nowhere have racial categories been built into the ideological and institutional fabric of modern societies. The two most obvious examples which did build in such categories, the Slave South of the United States and Nazi Germany, were both destroyed in conflicts with enemies for whom their racial practices had become unacceptable.

The situation becomes muddier still when we consider that much of the literature restricts itself to considerations of European racism or, to be blunt, white racism about black people. This is understandable: the predominant powers in modern times have been 'white', and 'white' states and societies have been culturally predominant, not merely in the fields of science and technology but also popular culture, as a result of the global use of the English language. But this hardly warrants the idea that thinking in racial categories is somehow a peculiarly Western disease, what the Indian scholar Dipesh Chakrabarty calls 'something the white people do to us'. Not only is this implausible, it verges on deliberate falsification. The most cursory observation of social behaviours around the world suggests that racial and ethnic attitudes are hardly restricted to Europeans or 'white' people. Two of the world's largest countries and homes to great civilisations, China and India, provide plentiful evidence of widespread assumptions of racial superiority and inferiority, now and in the past. Traditional Chinese culture admired fairer skin tones associating them with intellect and female beauty, while (as elsewhere) the darker complexions of manual workers and peasants were associated with low economic and cultural status. While any public expression of such attitudes was suppressed during the revolutionary Maoist period, when the Chinese Communist Party proclaimed solidarity with the non-Western world, recent changes in China have seen the resurgence of racial prejudice. Indeed, virtually the only forms of mass social protest before the Tiananmen Square demonstrations of 1989 were Chinese student protests against African students. Recent surveys of Chinese opinion, even among the more educated sections of Chinese society, suggest very negative views of Africans. Similar phenomena can be found in India. There have been numerous incidents in India in which African students and others are racially abused and which have led African governments to complain to the Indian authorities at the highest level. Even among Indians there are forms of discrimination that, while we might not wish to call them racist, look rather similar, concerning 'caste' and 'untouchability'.

SLAVERY

If racism has come to seem a peculiarly arbitrary and awful form of oppression, one practice that it encouraged and justified has come to represent that oppression at its most unspeakable, namely the practice of slavery. While 'race' remains a social reality, and even colonialism, though fading from living memory, retains a presence, the institution of slavery has all but disappeared. It is fashionable to dispute this last point, and while it is true that in certain corners of the world practices continue that are reminiscent of slavery, people now use the term very broadly to indicate coercion. (Some estimates include the inmates of North Korean prison camps, some include forced marriages, and so on.) Part of the difficulty here is that the term 'slavery' has been used to describe a huge variety of forms of coercion throughout history. Slavery in the southern United States was massively different from slavery as practised in Ancient Rome. It is true that various forms of coerced or semi-coerced labour still exist, but slavery as a legitimate institution has disappeared. It is illegal everywhere and there are, for example, no official slave markets. The very fact that the term 'slavery' has been stretched to breaking point ('wage slavery', 'debt slavery') suggests that people are trading on the historical baggage. In any case, in the African context it is the historical experience that people have in mind.

As with colonialism and race, this story comes with a variety of themes and degrees of sophistication. Let's look briefly at two. John Locke, the seventeenth-century English political philosopher, is widely regarded as a founding thinker of liberalism who did much to make freedom a central value in the Western political tradition. Yet he was also a man of practical affairs, concerned among other things with questions of trade and Britain's early colonial expansion in America. He was an important member of the Board of Trade and an investor in a number of colonial and trading ventures. Scholarly research has shown that in this role he at least condoned slavery. But if John Locke condoned slavery, how can he be a theorist of freedom? And further, given his importance in the Western political tradition, how can that tradition lay claim to freedom as a central value? Doesn't this suggest that the Western tradition is hypocritical, saying one thing and doing another?

There is a link between this kind of rather arcane historical research and wider public debate. Unlike many other areas of scholarly enquiry, considerable sums of money are available for research into every aspect of the Atlantic slave trade, and a very large number of publications are produced about it for every kind of audience. Beyond research and publication, the slave trade is commemorated widely and publicly, most recently by the United Nations which, since 2007, has declared 25 March to be an International Day of Remembrance of the Victims of Slavery and the Transatlantic Slave Trade. In March 2015, the United Nations unveiled a monument with the same name in the visitors' plaza at UN Headquarters.

What do the debate about John Locke and the United Nations monument have in common? They both focus exclusively on the Atlantic slave trade and slavery in the Americas, as does a huge proportion of the scholarly and popular literature. Much of the earlier writing about slavery and the slave trade gloried in recounting the gruesome, playing on the themes of 'tight packing', 'monstrous' rates of mortality and 'cheap' slaves bought for virtually nothing. While early exaggerations have recently been modified by new research, the facts remain sobering. Estimates vary as to the number of Africans shipped across the Atlantic, but in the eighteenth and nineteenth centuries the figure is likely to be somewhere between 12.5 and 14 million. From further back, say from 1500, the figure is possibly as high as 18 million. Mortality rates were high, especially given that most slaves were generally young and healthy, though they slowly declined in the eighteenth century. Revolts were often bloodily suppressed. Slaves were condemned to short lives of unrelenting toil, deprived of virtually all dignity, physical comforts or rights. Sugar cropping in the southern United States was probably one of the most intense labour coercion systems ever designed. Slaves were constantly exposed to the threat of arbitrary violence. However, there is an obvious difficulty with the mainstream story that all but its most vehement promoters acknowledge, if on occasion somewhat reluctantly. As the United Nations points out on its own website, the slave trade, and later slavery as an institution, were abolished by Western states (the leading role being played by Great Britain) in response to political agitation in those same states, itself animated by a variety of ideas and concepts in the Western tradition. An important source of such ideas (though by no means the only one) was John Locke, whose remarks about slavery simply cannot be used to justify slavery even as it was practised in his own time, though it seems likely that towards the end of his life he turned a blind eye because of other political priorities. In any case, if Locke's writing provides such useful support for slavery, it is surely odd that the staunchest defenders of plantation slavery in the southern United States never drew on his writings for such a purpose, whereas their enemies, seeking to emancipate slaves and abolish the institution, frequently did.

There is a second context which should give us pause. Let's

return to the United Nations memorial where we can read that 'some African kings were complicit in facilitating the sale of African captives'. This is, to say the least, something of an understatement. Not only was this slave trade organised by Africans but the practice of slavery itself was widespread in Africa. Up until the middle of the nineteenth century Western knowledge of Africa was extremely limited, partly for geographical reasons, partly because of disease barriers, but mostly because a wide variety of African rulers were able to determine the conditions, political and commercial, under which they would deal with outsiders. Slave traders had to negotiate the purchase of slaves, they could not dictate terms, and they were required to wait on the coast for their human cargo to be brought to them. Everywhere, they had to pay some sort of local tax and abide by local rules and norms. Since securing a full complement of slaves often took time, traders were also dependent on local suppliers for water and other essentials. Indeed, what made the trade viable was that its conditions were enforced by African powers. The popular image of white slavers raiding into Africa is very wide of the mark. The transatlantic slave trade, however reprehensible, was a collaborative enterprise, so much so that many West African rulers were puzzled and angry when told that it was to be abolished.

Finally, we must acknowledge that the stress on the Atlantic slave trade in both popular and academic writing, although well meant, has had the effect of obscuring not only other slave trades, but also the simple fact that, however repugnant to modern sensibilities, historically slavery has been a widespread method of organising human labour. Africans were not just traded across the Atlantic; they were traded across the Sahara. The size of the Arab or Muslim slave trade is much more difficult to estimate than the transatlantic trade and fewer attempts has been made to do so, but some scholars suggest that between 650 CE and 1900, something like 13 million slaves were taken across the Sahara, the Red Sea and the Indian Ocean. But the Arab or Muslim trade was not the only other slave trade, and if even today it is relatively unknown, there was another which remains almost entirely unknown.

Britain ended its own participation in the slave trade in 1807 and subsequently embarked on a vigorous policy to persuade other powers to cease their participation. Such pressure usually consisted of treaties to allow for inspection of ships on the high seas. Only in exceptional circumstances did British governments in the nineteenth century resort to more robust methods. The most dramatic example of this occurred in 1816 when a substantial British fleet, with Dutch support, bombarded an important slaving city. It was the largest bombardment of any onshore target by a naval force during the age of sail, and British seamen suffered a higher rate of casualties than they experienced at Trafalgar. The city was Algiers, and as a result Britain secured the release of some four thousand slaves. These slaves were European, though none were British, captured by North African slavers in the Mediterranean. This slave trade had also been going on for centuries, and it is even more difficult to estimate the numbers involved, but a leading authority suggests that they may have amounted to some million persons between the sixteenth to eighteenth centuries. Before the eighteenth century, some of those kidnapped and enslaved were British. When James Thomson wrote 'Rule, Britannia!' in 1740, which includes the famous line 'Britons never will be slaves', people knew exactly what he meant. Nor should we suppose that the conditions of capture or servitude were any better than in the transatlantic trade: some estimates suggest mortality rates at 20%, and conditions of servitude, especially on the galleys, were at least as grim as plantation work. Yet it has been called the 'invisible trade', and there are no proposals for monuments to its victims.

'THEY LEFT US NOTHING BUT OUR RESENTMENT'

Colonialism, race and slavery: these three themes can be woven together to tell an extraordinarily powerful story, a story which for many people, even today, remains compelling beyond the complications of historical controversies and political disputes. When this story first emerged, on the eve of decolonisation, it made possible a whole new way of presenting Africa. Far from having been a place of little progress, or 'backwardness', or even a place 'without history', Africa could now be seen as the equal of anywhere else, and Africans as the equals of everyone else. Far from being developed, however inadequately, by colonial rule, Africa could now be seen as a place where such rule had in fact obstructed the very possibility of progress. And far from acknowledging the usefulness of contact with the West, such contact could be seen as a kind of abuse for which they were entitled to compensation. As Ghana's first president, Kwame Nkrumah, put it, 'They left us nothing but our resentment.'

But to make a politically effective story the raw material of such large themes needed to be sharpened, to be made more real, more accessible. The abstract assertion of human equality was, by the 1950s, hardly controversial, at least outside the ranks of the wilfully prejudiced. What was required was something much more emotionally rewarding, something that many, perhaps all, organised human societies have needed, and created – namely a sense of history. If eminent historians like Professor Hugh Trevor-Roper (one time Regius Professor of History at the University of Oxford) could say silly things like there was no African history, other historians felt duty-bound to refute such assertions.* This effort counterbalanced the negative or

---

* Trevor-Roper, H., 'The rise of Christian Europe', *The Listener*, LXX, 1809 [28 November 1963], pp. 871–5.

dismissive accounts of African history, but much of it lapsed into claims to greatness by way of association.

African history was glorified and packaged to meet the needs of African regimes. Many writers sought to discover in African history all the large cities, written scripts, advanced technologies and political organisation that (supposedly) were the hallmarks of progress everywhere. One way to do this was to locate their cultural histories in a more privileged civilisational process. There were furious debates as to whether ancient Egypt should be seen as part of Black Africa rather than as a distinct civilisation. A similar attempt to cash in on supposedly glorious periods of history led Kwame Nkrumah to rename the old colony of Gold Coast 'Ghana'. There was indeed a great empire of Ghana between the ninth and thirteenth centuries, but it was nowhere near modern Ghana and, more to the point, it held no resonance for modern Ghanaians. With the important exception of Ethiopia, there were virtually no political continuities between historic African polities and modern African states.

However, romanticised historical accounts were a politically appealing response to colonial rule and Africa's contact with the West more generally. If there had been a glorious historical past, that past must have been ruined, those achievements undermined, that history deliberately denigrated and denied. But in practice, while a glorious history might provide a warm glow, it proved very difficult to make any real connection with those pasts to make them politically and culturally useful. With the passage of time after independence, and the all too visible decline in many aspects of African life and living standards, the idea of a glorious past provided less and less comfort. How then to explain their own lack of progress? The answer lay readily to hand. There was a baleful 'colonial legacy' that blighted the possibility of progress. The same idea is behind 'neocolonialism' and (more recently) 'postcolonialism'. This idea of a colonial legacy could be elaborated in many ways, as an explanation for economic stagnation, ethnic antagonism or political instability. The effects of colonialism on independent African states are complex, and they continue to be the subject of serious debate – we may never have definitive answers. But, all too often, without refinements or qualifications, the idea of a colonial legacy has become a simplistic substitute for serious thought, an all-purpose explanation for anything that happened in post-independence Africa – indeed, an all-purpose explanation for the failure of African states and societies to develop.

In reality, nobody in post-independence Africa seriously imagined that there could be a return to historical traditions, and the idea of a 'colonial legacy' could not do much more than point out what the colonial powers had failed to do or, at best, how colonial rule made it more difficult to do what needed to be done. Neither of these offered much by way of a guide to action, but they did provide concrete pointers as to what others should do. The denigration of Africa, the enslavement of its people, the brutal nature of colonial conquest and rule, and the hindering of its progress all pointed towards the moral desirability of compensation for past misdeeds, as well as assistance in the future.

The romanticisation of history, the all-purpose explanation of the colonial legacy, and the endlessly flexible notion of compensation were the main ways in which the big themes of race, colonialism and slavery were developed. It remains to explore how this story worked politically, and to ask questions about who benefits from this portrayal, not only in a material sense, but more broadly in a way that encompasses psychological or emotional compensations.

Virtually overnight, colonial rule changed from being a noble if endlessly flawed project, to being evil almost beyond imagining, on a par, as its detractors continue to argue, with slavery and even genocide. For the perpetrators of this awfulness, Western states and peoples, the burden of guilt became almost unbearable. It was only natural that people would look for a narrative that provided both repentance and the chance to make amends. The new picture of Africa did precisely that. Psychologically it provided some relief from the burden of guilt, a confession that terrible wrongs had been committed and were now acknowledged. But it also promised redemption: a new ethical imperative which pointed the way to concrete action, to objectives that could actually be achieved, which in turn would go some way to atone for past sins. The main agency of this ethical imperative was African nationalism. Labouring under the burden of guilt, Western opinion-formers chose not to see African nationalism as a political programme like any other, rooted in a particular set of political and cultural circumstances and necessarily riven with all sorts of inconsistencies and compromises. Whereas by the second half of the twentieth century nationalism was widely viewed, in the words of one eminent scholar, as the 'starkest political shame of the age', African nationalism, in the words of another, was an excellent and positive thing.* Practice followed belief. African nationalist leaders were feted, praise was heaped on their 'charisma', their wisdom, their commitments to 'nation-building'. Nationalist propaganda was widely reported as truth. The United Nations blithely appointed nationalist movements as 'sole representatives' of their people. In doing all this, Western opinion formers could feel that past wrongs were being righted, and that they were helping the people who would build a new future for Africa.

For African nationalist movements and their leaders, the benefits of the new story of Africa were almost incalculable. They could draw on the idea of a glorious history in general terms, for example in various versions of pan-Africanism. But they

---

* Dunn, J., *Western Political Theory in the Face of the Future* (Cambridge: Cambridge University Press, 1979), p. 55; R. Emerson quoted in Young, C., 'Nationalism, ethnicity and class in Africa', *Cahiers d'Etudes Africaines*, XXVI–3, 1986, pp. 421–95 at p. 425.

could also locate themselves in a history of resistance to colonial conquest and rule. Western historians readily provided schemas that linked what they called 'primary resistance' to colonial rule to modern African nationalism. They cast colonial history in racial terms and helpfully obscured the ways in which race was not always a unifier on either side of the colonial divide. The idea of a 'colonial legacy' neatly captured Africa's relative lack of development; it also highlighted the role of the new African elites in overcoming it. Not merely overcoming it, but doing so with extraordinary speed – 'like jet propulsion' – as Kwame Nkrumah famously put it.*

To make these points is not to criticise African nationalism or its leaders. In politics, as no doubt in life, you must play the cards you have been dealt. The African leaders actually played their cards rather well, and in the main secured peaceful transitions to independence on good terms. So in those heady days of decolonisation, when Kenyan politician Tom Mboya told the West to 'scram from Africa', Africa's leaders could be forgiven for not reflecting too hard on the disadvantages of the various ideas they had used to such good political effect.

But the time would come when it could no longer be denied that Africa's glorious history was rather more complex than it had seemed and that, if anything, the mainstream story obscured the difficulties and complexities of social change. The passage of time would also throw increasing doubt on any simple idea of a 'colonial legacy', and it would become clear that the idea could turn from a handy explanation of difficulties into a permanent excuse for failure. At that time, hardly anyone foresaw that compensation might become, not a means to a better world, but rather a crutch, almost a substitute for that better world. But the new story of Africa would work for a good while yet.

---

* Nkrumah, K., *Autobiography* (Nelson, 1957), p. x.

2

$22,000 FOR EIGHTEEN CUPS OF TEA

WITH THE EXCEPTION OF SOUTHERN AFRICA, the European powers scrambled out of Africa even faster than they had scrambled into it. Within ten years of Ghana's independence in 1957, some thirty more African countries had also become independent. In the wake of the Second World War the very idea of the domination of other peoples had simply rotted away. African elites had demanded for their countries, and were granted, exactly the same attributes of statehood possessed by other states: mutual recognition by other states, the conventions and practices of diplomacy, membership of the United Nations, and participation in international law. There was, however, one special feature of African independence which might be called the 'development bargain'. On the one hand, African elites would vigorously pursue the project of 'development' that the colonial powers had so conspicuously failed to achieve. On the other hand, and in order to assist such a project, Western states (not just the old colonial powers) would transfer to them resources which came to be known as foreign or development aid. In a nutshell, the Africans promised rapid progress and the West promised to fund a substantial part of that progress. While the details of the aid relationship would see much refining and would go through many different phases, its political core remained the same – to atone for the past and to complete the task of modernising a continent.

THE COMING OF AID

Some people suggest that post-independence aid to Africa was simply a different form of exploitation, fashioned to secure economic predominance by the colonial powers over their old possessions by indirect means, rather than through direct political control. Others argue that the new phenomenon of aid was, and indeed still is, just another weapon in the disputes between the great powers to secure the allegiance of weaker ones. We can call these explanations 'aid as interest' or 'aid as power'. There is some truth in them, particularly the use of aid as power during the ideological battles of the Cold War. The Akosombo Dam in Ghana (built in the early 1960s), which created the largest artificial lake in the world, was substantially funded by Britain and the United States (as well as the World Bank). When it was first actively considered it was to be linked to an aluminium smelter because the price of aluminium was high and could justify the expansion of capacity. But it was also funded because the donors believed large infrastructure projects were crucial for economic development. They also feared the Soviet Union and China might finance it. In this case, as in others, they saw themselves engaged in a battle for influence with the communist powers throughout the newly developing world, and aid was a weapon in that battle. The United States and Britain were particularly concerned because of a previous dispute with Egypt over the construction of the Aswan Dam across the Nile, which the Egyptian government regarded as fundamental for the country's development. The USSR had offered the Egyptian government arms supplies as well as the financing of the dam, and used these as a way of extending Soviet influence in the Middle East. What such cases show is that, as always in politics, motives are mixed and their precise mix is not always clear, either to analysts or participants.

While economic and strategic calculations played a role in aid, they do not provide the best explanation of the way it developed over time. First, we have to acknowledge the continuities between the colonial and postcolonial periods. Towards the end of the colonial period virtually all the colonial powers had begun to increase both the resources and the personnel devoted to the economic development, and to some extent the welfare, of African populations. Part of this involved economic planning which, although rather limited, was a considerable break with previous practice. Both the Akosombo and the Aswan dams had been envisaged, and some planning had started, in the colonial period. Newly independent African states often adopted, more or less without alteration, colonial economic plans, and often encouraged expatriate personnel to remain to help implement them. It was not unusual for African governments to continue projects their leaders had only recently denounced as 'colonial oppression'. The fact that colonial officials were often asked to stay on, and that they often wanted to, suggests that 'oppressors' was not a complete description of their role, even in colonial times. There were good arguments for maintaining these continuities as most African countries had little by way of a business class, and minimal administrative experience, and borrowing from colonial plans helped to reinforce appeals for further economic aid. These continuities suggest why, more than half a century after their retreat, the old colonial powers still give priority to their erstwhile colonial territories. Most British (and Irish) aid goes to Anglophone Africa, most French aid to Francophone Africa. Germany lost its colony of South West Africa (now Namibia) in 1919; a century later it is still Namibia's largest foreign aid donor, and it is not easy to see what great advantages it derives from this role. On balance, then, aid looks less like the ruthless calculation of economic and political advantage, rather more like historical inertia and a sense of obligation.

A second set of reasons why sceptical accounts of aid are not very convincing is that from quite early on Western states began to set targets for aid, though most donors fell short of these targets. The UN General Assembly in 1970 called for 0.7% of rich countries' GDP to be devoted to aid, a number based on long discussions. The richer countries accepted this target in principle, although many of them failed to attain it. Some countries, notably the Scandinavian countries and Holland, attained the target quite quickly, and even exceeded it. Among major powers, only Britain has also recently reached this threshold. Most of the countries that have reached the threshold had no colonial ties with Africa, which also suggests that aid was felt to be a general obligation on richer states, rather than an instrument of statecraft. Some groups of countries, notably the European Union, have committed themselves to extensive aid programmes of a multilateral kind to which all member states contribute as part of their membership, whether the contributions are 'in their interests' or not. So aid was in many ways a collective enterprise of (mostly) Western states, managed through new kinds of international organisations. The most important of these was the World Bank which, although it was ultimately controlled by the 'great powers', sought to carve out a space for itself in the postwar international order. But other organisations came to have important roles in the aid enterprise, notably the International Monetary Fund (IMF) and the specialised agencies of the United Nations.

Leaving all this aside, the increasing weight of public opinion simply cannot be understood as self-interested. That opinion was partly rooted in a Christian tradition of generosity and fellow feeling. It was the World Council of Churches in 1958 which had called for the rich countries to donate 1% of their GDP in aid, rather than the 0.7% that was finally agreed. Whether in religious or secular form, the values of human equality were asserted with renewed vigour after the barbarisms of the Second World War. Nor was this purely rhetorical. In most Western countries commitments to equality had increasingly taken real institutional form in the postwar 'welfare state' whose core idea was one of common entitlements due to everyone. It seemed obvious to many that such entitlements should, at least eventually, be extended beyond national boundaries to everyone across the globe. In an age of astonishing technological achievement, basic poverty seemed increasingly intolerable. Much of this feeling was vague, sentimental, often oblivious to real economic and political forces, and only intermittently expressed. We might compare it with anti-slavery sentiment in the nineteenth century, which was also often ill-informed and inconsistent, but nonetheless a significant factor in politics. That sentiment was the fuel for a small number of people who used it to focus pressure on governments. Governments often turned a blind eye, and they might refuse to act in certain circumstances, but they could not consistently ignore the weight of public opinion on the slavery issue. Much the same dynamic has applied to aid. An increasingly well-funded and well-organised network of groups has been a major factor in the consistent support for aid to Africa. In those countries with the highest levels of aid donation there has been, until very recently, a national consensus on the desirability of aid.

There were also a number of other, more practical arguments, that made aid attractive. Two particular features of the postwar experience made aid seem not only morally right but also practically plausible. The first was a widespread view that the Second World War had in large part been caused by economic factors, whether these were economic difficulties within states or economic rivalries between them. If that view was right then an important way of avoiding a potential nuclear conflict in the future was to ensure a much wider degree of economic growth and equality. Second, aid seemed to work and work quickly. After all, Europe had been devastated by the Second World War both in human and physical terms. The US Marshall Plan, consisting of immediate assistance to kick-start the European economies, though its importance may have been exaggerated somewhat at the time, undoubtedly played a role in reviving economic growth. By the early 1950s, Europe was booming again. The parallels with Europe seemed obvious: Africa needed roads, schools and health systems; foreign aid could help to provide them. Though there were debates about which of these areas were the main priority, it seemed obvious that rapid development would follow financial aid.

MAKING SENSE OF AID

But what exactly is 'aid'? There have been endless disputes about this question. The important thing about definitions is not whether they are true, but what people are doing with them. Carol Lancaster, a prominent writer on aid who was involved in the US aid administration at the highest levels, defines it as a 'voluntary transfer of public resources, from a government to another government, to an NGO, or to an international organisation...with at least a 25% grant element, one goal of which is to better the human condition in the country receiving the aid'.*

---

*   Lancaster, C., *Foreign Aid: Diplomacy, Development, Domestic Politics* (Chicago: University of Chicago Press, 2008), p. 9. She notes immediately that while this is close to the definition of overseas development assistance used by the DAC (the Development Assistance Committee comprising all the Western countries that give aid) it differs significantly

This definition presents a whole series of ambiguities: Who gives aid? (States? Organisations? Individuals?) Who gets aid? (States? Groups? People?) What forms does aid take? (Money? Grants? Loans? Food? Training?) What are the purposes of aid? ('Relief'? 'Development'?)

For our purposes, let's say aid is defined as a set of resources provided by richer countries to poorer countries on concessional terms (so at least better than market rates). As it is meant to help people, it excludes military resources and private financial flows. On this basis we can classify aid into three basic types. The first, most visible examples are humanitarian supplies of food, medicine and shelter in the wake of disasters. In these cases the issue is unambiguous (a devastating loss of the means of life) and the need both pressing and obvious (clean water, food, medicines). Second, and not quite as obvious, is what is termed 'project aid', where resources are devoted to a particular concrete goal, be it schools, clinics, dams or bridges, usually involving physical infrastructure, but often also the supplies to keep them working (books, medicines, equipment, training). These are the kinds of projects that NGOs concentrate on, though states and international agencies do use them as well. Third, and least visible, are financial resources, either 'programme aid', where donors give money to states to spend as they see fit (though there may be strings attached), or debt relief, where states (and sometimes private agencies) write off debt so that countries no longer have to repay the principal and are relieved of interest payments.

Aid has been delivered by a number of different agencies from the beginning, but the relationships between them have changed

---

in two ways. First, the DAC definition only includes transfers to low-income countries (so excludes financial aid to countries like Israel); and, second, the DAC definition includes anything that might make things 'better' – humanitarian relief say – rather than limiting it to 'development', meaning (roughly) economic growth leading to the reduction of poverty.

over time. States have always been the main providers. Other agencies include international organisations like the agencies of the United Nations (UNICEF, WHO and so on), but also groups of states like the European Economic Community, later the European Union. Although the budgets of these organisations are funded by states, member states don't directly control their policies. Next, there are what from the 1950s were called non-governmental organisations (NGOs), which are often funded by individual donors. Confusingly, many of the bigger NGOs have, in recent years, increasingly been financed by states. Lastly, we should note that in the last ten years or so private philanthropy has become an important aid provider, especially in Africa. This is either formally organised (e.g. the Bill & Melinda Gates Foundation) or associated with wealthy individuals, often from the world of entertainment.

Over time, aid has become more multilateral. States continue to be central and they provide the bulk of the resources, but they increasingly share the aid project with international organisations and NGOs. What has emerged is a complex web of influences and relationships around the idea and the practice of aid. States encouraged the development of certain kinds of NGOs, but they also found that NGOs could bring pressure to bear on them through public opinion. Although the United Nations cannot impose conditions on its members, it tends to set standards in areas such as health and labour policies. The UN can also mobilise international public opinion, for example in designating the 1960s and 1970s 'development decades'. For their part, NGOs found the UN a useful forum to lobby for funds and bring pressure to bear on member states to increase their aid budgets. But as states spent more of their aid resources through NGOs, they also insisted on having more influence on the way those resources were spent. States ultimately do control the United Nations, the World Bank and the IMF, and if they are determined, they can impose their agendas on these international organisations. But in practice international organisations and NGOs almost always have some room for manoeuvre.

The entanglement of relationships between these organisations led to an increasing professionalisation of the aid business. The impetus for aid may have been rooted in sympathy and guilt, but as it gathered momentum, and especially as it made greater and greater demands for resources in the late 1950s and early 1960s, aid agencies increasingly felt the need to flesh out their rationales and policies. The United States Agency for International Development (USAID), the French Ministry for Cooperation and Development, and the German Ministry of Cooperation, were all set up in 1961. The British Labour government in 1964 created a Ministry of Overseas Development. All these new agencies pulled together various kinds of aid that had hitherto been dispersed across different departments. The major capitalist countries, which had already grouped themselves into the Organisation for Economic Co-operation and Development to oversee the Marshall Plan, formed a Development Assistance Committee in 1961 to focus attention on, gather information about and make recommendations concerning development. The World Bank, the IMF and the UN Development Programme are all observer members of this committee. The United Nations also set up an Economic Commission for Africa in 1958, and the United Nations Development Programme (UNDP) in 1965, merging together a number of previous smaller UN programmes. Its first head was an American, Paul Hoffman, who had run the Marshall Plan. Non-government and research organisations quickly emerged to contribute to the debate. The UK's Overseas Development Institute was founded in 1960. In the US, the Ford and Rockefeller Foundations set up and funded the Overseas Development Council in 1969.

All these, and other organisations, contributed to a flood of policy statements and discussion papers about development. Development Economics and Development Studies became university subjects. But the general drift of these documents was remarkably consistent. One of the most important, the Pearson Report published in 1969, gave recommendations that would continue to be repeated for the next half century. These included the need to make trade freer and more equitable, to promote flows of private direct investment, to increase development aid, and to make it more coherent, less tied, and more of a partnership.*

All these agencies were in the business of giving money, and over time this developed into a substantial activity. Events like the oil crisis of the early 1970s, or famines in parts of Africa in the mid-1970s and 1980s, triggered surges in assistance of various kinds. But aid volumes were also shaped by longer-term shifts in development doctrines and fashions, as well as increasingly effective publicity campaigns run by NGOs which played on the anxieties and guilt of Western publics.

Over time, there were huge increases in the rate of giving. Danish aid tripled in the late 1960s, as did German aid in the early 1970s. While there were some variations between donors, aid was given on an increasingly concessional basis, either in the form of outright grants, or loans at very low rates of interest with long repayment periods. In addition, the practice of 'tied aid', which required receiving countries to purchase from suppliers in donor countries, and was common at the beginning of the aid era, steadily declined to less than a third by the 1980s (and has continued to decline since). The focus shifted towards poverty, replacing the emphasis on infrastructure that had characterised the 1960s and 1970s. The motto on the wall of the World Bank in Washington is 'Our dream is a world free of poverty.' And although aid flowed to other parts of the world, almost from the beginning of the aid era it went disproportion-

---

* There are similar kinds of arguments in later similar reports, such as the Brandt Commission (1980) and the South Commission (1990), but a common feature was a stress on development as a global responsibility.

ately to Africa. In 1965, Africa was receiving around 20% of Western aid. The Nordic countries and the Netherlands channelled at least half their aid to Africa. By the 1980s, the African share of aid per person was higher than anywhere else in the developing world. The global totals involved were impressive. The Organisation for Economic Co-operation and Development (OECD) countries had, by 1990, probably ploughed $50–60 billion into Africa; some analysts argue considerably more. Repeated predictions at that time that aid to Africa would decline, based on assumptions that aid was really about self-interest, proved wide of the mark: by 2005 the total aid provided to Africa by OECD countries had risen to $650 billion.

According to the Development Assistance Committee (DAC), about $1.3 trillion has flowed into the region from 1960 to 2012. The figures for individual states are equally striking. Between 1964 and 1994 the World Bank loaned Nigeria $7 billion. Between 1970 and 1999, donor funds to Kenya averaged about 9% of GDP, accounting for about 20% of the annual government budget and financing slightly over 80% of development expenditures. Aid to Tanzania went from $51 million in 1970, to $650 million in 1980. Between 1986 and 1990, Tanzania received some $850 million a year, about 80% of which was in the form of grants. Zaire, later the Democratic Republic of the Congo, received over $1 billion a year during the period 1960–90. In the 1980s alone, Somalia received some $2.5 billion. For decades, aid made up about half the Togo economy.

THE POLITICAL CONSEQUENCES OF AID

Once aid became plentiful the scene was set for the 'development bargain' to flourish. Both parties to the bargain assumed that large amounts of aid would bring about development, and fairly rapidly at that. Assessments were optimistic, and there was much talk of aid 'making itself obsolete' – even of economic 'takeoff'. Of course aid was used to provide bridges and roads, schools and hospitals, training programmes and financial resources of all kinds. So much of the aid debate concerned questions of causality and priority. Which forms of aid worked best? Was education more important than investment in agriculture? Was primary education more important than university education? But the overriding imperative to donate meant that other questions about the possible consequences of aid were largely ignored. There was considerable reluctance to contemplate the ways in which foreign aid might hinder development. One such way was that, far from benefiting 'the people', the resources supplied to African regimes and leaders enabled them to stay in power, irrespective of their commitments to development. A second way was that aid could bring about circumstances which in some ways actually undermined development.

Until the mid-1980s, most aid was project aid – dams and other development projects that drew on previous colonial experience. Very few African elites, while most of them were committed in some sense to 'development', had any very clear idea of how it was to be achieved, and there was even less clarity as to how aid resources should be used. So despite a widespread anti-Western rhetoric, most African regimes were happy to accept project proposals. Donors were keen to give aid and encouraged by the ease with which project proposals were accepted. This enthusiasm for aid went beyond the commitments announced in politicians' speeches and UN resolutions and percolated into the structures of aid agencies and the attitudes and perspectives of their staff. The biggest aid agency of all was (and still is) the World Bank, which was geared towards, as the saying had it, 'getting money out the door'. This apparently strange state of affairs was occasionally noted by the Bank itself, as in a report of 1992 which acknowledged that 'signals from senior management are consistently seen by staff to focus on lending targets rather than results on the ground".* Given this, the oversight of development projects was often very weak. The Bank, as well as most other donors, often overestimated the likely outcomes of development projects, and there was little attempt to independently assess their actual contribution to their stated goals, much less the broader goal of 'development'. The key thing was to get the money 'out the door', rather than actually figure out what was being done with it. So the most successful managers in aid agencies were those who could demonstrate that they could plan projects and persuade their organisation to authorise the funds. Managers did not pursue successful careers in the aid business by questioning the usefulness of projects or doubting the money spent on them. On the other hand, there were no significant disincentives either. Moving this money involved no risk; its promoters were not likely to be questioned either by the ultimate donors (the taxpayers), or by the supposed beneficiaries (who had little say). The same incentives and lack of disincentives applied to politicians in donor countries. Politicians could make grandiose claims and win political credit without being subject to much scrutiny. Quite the reverse – the story of 'success' was precisely what the public wanted to hear. Donors constantly asserted that African countries were 'improving', 'making progress', while rolling over debt or providing new loans.

The beneficiaries of aid were not slow to see the possibilities of such an organisational culture, and a variety of techniques developed to take advantage of it, ranging from forged invoices to overpricing. Quite frequently, officials set up shell companies which they themselves owned, or were connected with, in order to secure 'development' contracts. Much World Bank project money took the form of 'special accounts', funds allocated for

---

* World Bank, *Effective Implementation: Key to Development Impact* (Wapenhans Report) (Washington, DC: World Bank, 1992), p. 23.

day-to-day operations and deposited in local commercial banks, often in foreign exchange. These were open to various kinds of currency manipulation – for example, withdrawing US dollars, changing them into the local currency, then redepositing the funds at the official exchange rate. These special accounts often earned interest, and the proceeds of such accumulation were not accounted for. Funds allocated to, say, road-building, would in part be used to acquire vehicles or construct offices for which furniture and other supplies would be ordered. Technical assistance, involving training, attendance at seminars, workshops and the like, could be used to collect daily attendance allowances ('per diems'), even if there had been no attendance. Training can mean overseas trips, the acquisition of qualifications – one group of officials involved in a Ugandan rural development project managed to get 'trained' four times! The practice of ghost workers became widespread so that payrolls and budgets were inflated, salaries claimed, and then used for other purposes. Finally there is the diversion of goods themselves. Aid project funds could be used to purchase goods which are then sold on the open market or distributed through networks. Schoolbooks or medicines often never reached their intended beneficiaries but turned up for sale somewhere else. A Swedish researcher found that over the period 1990–5, about 13% of the aid allocated to schools in Uganda actually reached them. Next door, in Tanzania, only about 20% of aid funds provided for schoolbooks were reaching the schools. One World Bank official, checking the documentation on an aid project, found a claim for eighteen cups of tea costing $22,000. This project was deemed a success.

So as the aid system developed it provided numerous extraction points, most of which were controlled or influenced by senior politicians and officials. In circumstances where as much as half the state budget was provided virtually free by outsiders, access to political power was simultaneously access to wealth and status. Of course, some of the wealth of African elites derived from legitimate economic activities – Félix Houphouët-Boigny had been a successful farmer before he became president of Côte d'Ivoire. But even much of the legitimate business activity of the political class derived from its access to state power rather than any great entrepreneurial flair or careful accumulation. African political elites were notorious for accumulating vast fortunes, much of which would be held overseas, and enjoying opulent lifestyles. 'Emperor' Bokassa of the Central African Empire (now Republic) had a penchant for French property, with four chateaux in the country and a mansion in Paris, as well as houses in Nice and Toulouse. President Houphouët-Boigny built one of the largest churches in the world (modelled on St Peters in Rome) in his home village at a cost of $300 million. President Mobutu Sese Seko of Zaire turned his home village of Gbadolite into what was sometimes nicknamed the 'African Versailles', with not one but three palaces for his use, as well as an international airport and a nuclear bunker. President Siaka Stevens of Sierra Leone nearly bankrupted his country providing lavish accommodation for the Organisation of African Unity (OAU) Assembly in 1980. Kenya ran into a budget deficit funding the African Games in 1986. While much of this grandiose spending and accumulation was derived from the domestic economy, foreign aid was much easier to access and could be controlled by a few powerful individuals. It therefore formed part of a pool of resources that enabled African elites to enrich themselves and to entrench their political positions.

The most senior members of African elites took the lion's share, but these resources supported the lifestyle of the junior ranks of political elites. There were, at least initially, some genuine arguments for this. For many years, under colonial rule, Africans had been limited to the lower rungs of state employment. These discriminatory practices caused huge resentment, which postcolonial states would have found difficult to ignore. So, from the very beginning of independence, politicians and civil servants at the lower levels insisted, as a matter of justice, on pay parity with recently departed colonial administrators. But such principled arguments soon disappeared in the rush for the perks of office, the comfortable houses in the best parts of town, membership of exclusive clubs, special allowances for vehicles and so on. As René Dumont, a keen observer of post-independence Africa, noted as early as 1962, a National Assembly deputy in Gabon was paid more than a British MP. African parliamentarians are still, almost everywhere, some of the best paid people on the continent. In 1993 alone, the Ivory Coast National Assembly doubled the salaries of its members, during a time of extreme economic difficulty for the country as a whole. A recent report shows that four in five of the highest paid parliamentary representatives in the world are in Africa.

Even lower down the social hierarchy there were benefits to be had. Public sector employment expanded very rapidly in independent Africa. There were roughly three times as many people on the public payroll in Africa in the 1980s as there had been in the 1960s; indeed, the majority of wage earners were state employees. In Ghana, the public service expanded by 70% between 1960 and 1965. This came at a cost: in many African countries, well over half the national budget was spent on civil service pay. Even when the economic position of public sector workers deteriorated with the economic crises of the 1970s and 1980s, state employees were almost always considerably better off than other sections of the population. And part of the reason for that was the opportunity for graft and corruption.

The availability of aid did not necessarily encourage political consensus or elite cooperation; indeed, more often than not it had the reverse effect. Beyond self-enrichment, aid enabled African regimes to maintain a monopoly on power and under-mine or repress their opponents. African leaders loved to be photographed receiving cheques from donor agency officials. President Kamuzu Banda of Malawi regularly quoted the World

Bank to the effect that his regime was a 'star performer'. He routinely referred to Kamuzu's roads and Kamuzu's hospitals, although virtually every road and hospital in the country was built with foreign aid. Anyone wishing to use a hospital was required to be a member of the ruling party – the Malawi Congress Party (MCP). Equally, when President Moi took over in Kenya in 1982, the pattern of aid projects began to move towards his ethnic base in the west of the country. This trend applied not only to the Kenyan government's own resources (in the form of taxation etc.) but even to the distribution of foreign aid. Aid programmes were increasingly being transferred to project aid, to give donors greater control over spending. Despite all this, the Kenyan government managed to direct aid resources to the president's political base. On occasion the president personally decided where a road should be built, and he vetoed projects that might benefit his political opponents. What makes this even more remarkable is that in the late 1980s and early 1990s, relations between donors and the Kenyan government were antagonistic – donors had effectively forced President Moi to accept multiparty politics, and the US ambassador even claimed the Kenyan government had tried to kill him!

THE SOCIAL CONSEQUENCES OF AID

We might argue that, problematic though these developments were, they could be accepted as an unfortunate by-product of a basically sound process. Provided aid was getting to African societies and achieving 'development', a certain amount of 'leakage' could be tolerated. But there are other reasons, beyond the enrichment of African elites or the enhancement of their political power, why foreign aid could actually impede development processes in more fundamental ways. One of these is the phenomenon of 'aid dependency'.

Aid dependency can have a number of negative consequences: inflationary pressures that undermine exports (so-called 'Dutch disease'); a disincentive to collect taxes; shifting accountability from citizens to donors; stimulating rent-seeking and corruption. In the 1960s, the volume of aid to African countries as a percentage of GDP was around 2.5%, much the same as in South Asia. But by the mid-1990s a number of African countries relied on foreign aid for 30% of their GDP. Although aid dependence has declined in recent years, many countries still remain extremely dependent. Tanzania's aid dependency increased from 0.5% of GDP in 1970, to 17% in 1990, and is still around 10–15%. Almost no other countries in the world have experienced this level of aid dependence over a such a long period.

A second issue is the 'absorptive capacity' of countries: in relatively undeveloped economies there are all sorts of bottleneck problems concerning storage capacities, transport networks, or power supplies. Medicines may be supplied, even the refrigeration units to cool them, but without power the medicines will still spoil. Many development projects require subsequent maintenance for which resources may be in short supply. Skilled manpower of all kinds can also be in short supply. If projects are held up, financial resources can end up languishing in bank accounts. Absorbing aid requires a minimally competent state, a requirement that was conspicuously lacking in the vast majority of African states, certainly in the three decades or so after independence. Even with goodwill, most African states lacked the capabilities of measurement, planning and assessment, or the setting of policy priorities that many aid projects required.

Third, the influx of huge amounts of aid had deleterious consequences for policymaking in African states. The fact that a substantial part of public spending is provided, year after year, by outsiders, gives those outsiders considerable influence. But is it not a genuine influence in the sense of a cooperative commitment to a common project. Rather, if aid is a critical part of the state's resources, it becomes an influence that the beneficiaries of aid soon come to anticipate. So the mirror image of World Bank officials whose role is to get the money 'out the door', is African officials trying to attract money 'through the door'. Officials are rewarded, not for grappling with the questions of development, but rather for securing resources from donors. There is no point in questioning those who are trying to give you money, so policies are designed to attract their support, and to tell them what they want to hear.

But there is a further effect of aid that actively undermines development. If the severe limitations of the nascent African states were a huge obstacle to development, aid helped to make that obstacle even more entrenched. It is, of course, true that corruption and elite accumulation of wealth are perfectly compatible with development and economic growth. A glance at eighteenth-century England or the nineteenth-century United States reveals societies that were, certainly by modern standards, deeply corrupt. But this argument also misses something very important. To see this we have to stand back a little and consider how states come to acquire the capacity to regulate societies. Modern states are extremely expensive. In the past, this was because of frequent wars involving larger and more technologically sophisticated forces. Even now, major states still expend considerable resources on armaments, although the bulk of their resources are devoted to more peaceful ends. As states consolidate and expand, they need to raise revenue. One of the first ways states expanded was to increase their capacity to raise tax. Much of eighteenth-century England was corrupt, but even then one of the most efficient parts of the British state machinery was Excise.

As the demands of the state grew, states invented new ways to broaden the tax base by taxing the masses. It was no longer a simple question of taxing existing activity but stimulating the economic activity that would provide revenue. So at first, states tried to stimulate trade. Later, they sought to tax a whole range of economic transactions, and eventually began to tax everyone's income. Once they were subject to taxation, populations begin to demand more from their governments. What emerged was an implicit bargain: in exchange for the support of citizens, states must offer something in return. Initially this meant a degree of security – protection from invasion and the maintenance of public order. With time this 'social contract' developed into something like the modern welfare system. Usually what emerged was some sort of representative institution which mediated between rulers and people. Such institutions were emphatically not 'democratic' in the modern sense (although modern parliaments developed from them), but they did make it possible to hammer out bargains between different social groups.

Colonial states did try to tax their African populations, but they were not very successful at it. It was difficult to organise, expensive to administer, and of course they lacked the kind of political legitimacy that underpinned taxation of income. It was much easier to tax trade in ports and markets, which was what they did (although in some parts of British colonial Africa, particularly landlocked territories, greater efforts were made to collect direct taxes). Newly independent African states inherited this situation, and though they possessed greater legitimacy than colonial states, they faced the same difficulties of administration and cost. As that legitimacy eroded solving those problems became more difficult, and so they also tended to fall back on trade taxes. Unlike colonial states, however, they had access to another stream of resources, a stream of external revenue which greatly reduced the pressure on them to tax the domestic resources of their economies. These resources were provided by foreign actors with no standing in local society; they were often substantial and went directly to the state; relatively few people had control over them; and many people could benefit from distributing them.

It is easy to see how the virtuous cycle of taxation turns vicious with aid. First, African states had less incentive to find ways to tax domestic resources. As a result, they had less incentive to stimulate domestic economic activity to produce more wealth that could be taxed. Second, it reduced the pressure on elites to engage in social bargains with the wider population, and therefore obviated the need to engage with any kind of representative institution. With free resources at their disposal, the tendency of any elite is to buy off opposition, rather than pursue more politically sophisticated arrangements involving mediation between social groups and the construction of a public interest. The effect on the wider population is usually a profound political alienation. People who get very little from 'their' state, even basic security, will also pay little towards it, expect little from it and, if at all possible, avoid it.

The aid system as it developed for some thirty-five years after independence was then a double-edged sword. The donors wanted to give aid for the right reasons. There were, of course, other factors in play – sometimes power, sometimes economic interests. Nor can there be any doubt that, as it developed, the aid system was marred by all sorts of failings, incompetence, mistakes and so on. The African elites also wanted to bring about development, again largely for good reasons, to cultivate a higher standard of living and to take their place in a world of equal peoples and cultures. There were, of course, other factors in play – politicians everywhere are ambitious, and there was money to be made for new elites. They had little experience, and inevitably mistakes were made. But the aid system was set up in a way that led to outcomes nobody had intended. It was too indulgent on the donor side, and too open to manipulation on the beneficiary side. We have seen in this chapter how it could go wrong. But to see why it went wrong, and so badly, we must turn to the political circumstances that shaped Africa's post-independence trajectory.

3

TURNING A BLIND EYE

O N 21 MARCH 1960, AT A black township called Sharpeville, about fifty miles south of Johannesburg South Africa, sixty-seven people demonstrating outside a police station against 'pass' laws restricting the movement of Africans were shot dead by police, some in the back. The dead included eight women and ten children. Within hours the news reverberated around the world. It rapidly became a symbol of the brutality of the South African government and the system of apartheid it had imposed on the non-European population. It galvanised what was to become a global campaign against apartheid and gradually mobilised huge international pressure on white South Africa. The UN Security Council passed a resolution condemning the South African government, and the day continues to be marked by UNESCO. It has been comprehensively documented, studied, and commented on. Some twelve years later in Burundi, a small country in central Africa, over a period of three to four months, at least 100,000 people (possibly 200,000) of the Hutu ethnic group were massacred by the Tutsi-controlled army and militia groups. The dead included virtually the whole of the educated

Hutu population. In contrast to Soweto, there was no condemnation or even discussion at the United Nations; indeed the outside world more or less ignored these events. The Organisation of African Unity sent messages of support to the Burundi president, whose forces were organising the massacres. Since this episode there have been no international memorials, though there were one or two enquiries and reports some considerable time after the events.

How can we explain the dramatic differences between these two cases? What makes the slaughter of sixty-seven black South Africans so much more significant, both then and now, than the slaughter of 100,000 black Burundians? We can point to many contextual factors. South African apartheid was explicitly based on racial distinctions, and was so obviously a system of racial oppression that it could be easily grasped by any casual observer. The white population of South Africa (of both British and Dutch origin) made much of its participation in Western 'civilisation', and the country was a close ally of the major Western states and an enthusiastic participant in most international organisations. Yet its social and political structures increasingly deviated from what was acceptable to Western public opinion, making its claims to be part of the West increasingly implausible. Finally, South Africa was easily accessible to media organisations and therefore both highly visible and vulnerable to external pressure. The massacre of Hutus in Burundi, on the other hand, took place in a small, fairly obscure African state, not widely known or reported, certainly in the English-speaking world. The social and political dynamics of the country were complex and poorly understood. The factions were not so distinct in terms of the conditions of life. There were no Western states, nor even any activists in Western countries, angrily publicising and denouncing Tutsi domination in Burundi.

REPRESSION AND POLITICAL VIOLENCE

Perhaps more than any other factor, the difference between the two cases turned on race. In South Africa it was white policemen shooting black Africans, and in Burundi it was members of one African ethnic group killing members of another African ethnic group. The burden of guilt about Africa had allowed moral double standards that, looking back, seem so absurd as to be almost inexplicable. South Africa, for all its faults, attracted an extraordinary amount of attention from other states, international organisations and political movements, while much of what happened in the rest of sub-Saharan Africa remained virtually invisible, as in the Burundi case, or was explained away, rather than reflected on or accounted for. Much was made of the violence of colonial rule and of the violent responses to demands for freedom from that rule. Much less was made of the widespread violence and political repression of postcolonial Africa. Being an African politician in the thirty years or so after independence was probably one of the most dangerous occupations on the planet. One study of a sample of African political leaders in the thirty years after independence estimated that some 20% were executed, murdered, or died in prison. About 40% experienced imprisonment or exile. The study concluded that, since independence, somewhere between a half and two-thirds of the major politicians in sub-Saharan Africa have been imprisoned, exiled, or killed. It is rather more difficult to measure mass political violence, but one widely accepted study suggests that during the 1960s there were six episodes of violence with at least 10,000 civilian deaths, in the 1970s eight episodes, and in the 1980s nine episodes. None of these, incidentally, involved South Africa. And there were many more small-scale episodes of political violence. Many, if not most of them, were ignored at the time, and even today have attracted remarkably little study. Even generally peaceful countries, like Ghana, have not entirely escaped violent conflict.

Of course, some of the more grotesque cases did attract attention and occasionally condemnation. At their very worst, some kinds of political violence were little more than the whims of pathological leaders, who drew attention to themselves partly by virtue of their own buffoonery. Pride of place must go here to President Jean-Bédel Bokassa of the Central African Republic. Seizing power in a military coup in 1965, during which he personally killed his main rival, Bokassa ruled in an increasingly arbitrary fashion. He headed ten government departments himself, engaged in extraordinarily conspicuous consumption, and packed the armed forces, especially the Presidential Guard, with his own Mbaka people. His rule culminated in his self-proclamation in 1977 as emperor, in a ceremony modelled on that of Napoleon in 1804, which cost as much as the country's annual budget. Hardly less grotesque was the ruler of Equatorial Guinea in West Africa, Francisco Macías Nguema, elected in 1968, who repressed an attempted coup the following year, but from then on developed a murderous regime of terror which resulted in something like a third of the population fleeing the country. Ten of the twelve ministers in the first government were executed. Over 60% of the National Assembly deputies, and most senior civil servants, were murdered or driven into exile. In Uganda, General Idi Amin, having seized power in a coup in 1971, transformed himself into 'His Excellency President for Life Field Marshal Al Hadj Doctor Idi Amin Dada, VC, DSO, MC, Lord of All the Beasts of the Earth and Fishes of the Sea and Conqueror of the British Empire in Africa in General and Uganda in Particular'. Perhaps aiming to shore up his titles, he also attempted to lay claim the Scottish throne. During his years of power he instituted a reign of terror which led to the deaths of roughly 100,000 people in the first two years of his rule, and in some estimations around 250,000 by the time that rule ended. By a curious coincidence, all three of these regimes collapsed in 1979. Idi Amin, having attempted to invade Tanzania, was overthrown in the wake of Tanzanian retaliation. Macías Nguema was removed and executed in a coup organised by one of his nephews, while Bokassa had become so embarrassing even to his French patrons that they organised a coup to replace him.

In some ways it was the very absurdity of these regimes, and the rather lazy celebration of their demise, that allowed the deeper realities of African politics to be ignored. The Amins and the Bokassas could be treated as bizarre anomalies. This meant that not only did no other African state attract anything like the attention that South Africa did, they did not even attract the kind of unremitting international hostility shown towards the Pinochet regime in Chile after the 1973 coup which, over a couple of decades, may have murdered some 5,000 people.

It is important to remind ourselves about the extent of political violence and repression in postcolonial Africa, not least because it has by no means disappeared from parts of the continent, even today. But to make better sense of the forms that violence and repression in post-independence Africa took – to get beyond clichés – we need to address the development of African states. Although most African states made the transition to independence with some sort of democratic constitution in place, these were something of an afterthought, contrived by colonial powers already committed to a rapid withdrawal. These constitutions were given little time to embed themselves in local political realities. Within a few years of independence, virtually every state in Africa had abandoned its first constitution and replaced it with a more authoritarian form of government, usually labelled a 'one-party state'. In some ways reminiscent of the Leninist parties of the Soviet bloc, the one-party state maintained some democratic features (elections, a political party), but removed the element of open, free political competition. It has become fashionable in recent years to dismiss this form of state, and the arguments made for it, as nothing more than a veneer of self-justification for power-hungry elites; but this, I think, is a mistake. It is true that those in political power rarely go barefoot in any era, but that does not mean political power is always and only used in pursuit of a narrow self-interest. Just like the rest of us, political leaders are perfectly capable of acting from a variety of motives and not necessarily being entirely clear about what those motives are.

'IF YOU TRY TO INTERFERE WITH MY TASKS YOU WILL SEE THAT YOU WILL BE SMASHED'*

So why did virtually all the newly independent African states turn away from open political competition towards the one-party state? Why did African nationalist movements, and their leaders, think this was the most appropriate kind of state for their countries? They could make several quite cogent arguments for taking this step. There was widespread concern with the issue of national unity. Almost without exception, African countries were made up of an extremely wide range of social groups, marked by every kind of social, ethnic and religious difference. On top of that, as we have already noted, colonialism left its mark in a number of ways. Some areas and groups had prospered under colonial rule more than others. Some groups had acquired more education or had greater access to state employment. Despite their proclamations of unity, African leaders were acutely aware of these divisions within their societies and feared (with some justification) that those divisions might be exploited by forces outside the continent. The one-party state, with its emphasis on national identity, seemed the best way of dealing with these issues. Leaders also agreed on the priority of economic progress, and it was widely argued at the time that such progress required economic

---

* A Tanzanian official quoted in Van Freyhold, M., *Ujamaa Villages in Tanzania: An Analysis of a Socialist Experiment* (Portsmouth, NH: Heinemann, 1979), p. 185.

planning and a highly interventionist state. The one-party state seemed to promise that determined focusing of energies. Finally, proponents made the argument that nowhere in the world had countries achieved national unity and economic transformation under conditions of multiparty democracy. In this view, the question of 'development', in every sense, was such an over-whelming imperative that all energies had to be bent towards that end. The analogy was sometimes made with the practice, even in established democracies, of suspending normal politics during wartime. In such circumstances, opposition to the govern-ment is tantamount to treachery. As Tanzania's first president, Julius Nyerere, liked to say: 'Who could be against development?'

Not only did African leaders make these points, they attempted to apply them – even if fitfully in many places – to the business of ruling. In modern times, the 'business of ruling' means constructing a state, and that project, while difficult to do, is fairly well understood. Modern states consist of bureaucratic structures, organised hierarchies of officials with clearly defined functions, whose private interests are sharply separated from the public powers they have over other citizens. Their functions are clearly and publicly defined, and regulated by law. Modern states must be in some sense 'representative' of the wider society, and able to implement policies in the face of organised social interests. These general provisos are compatible with many different versions of the modern state (they certainly do not require mass democracy in the modern sense). But all modern states must be able to do three things: first, they have to be able to influence the wider society and shape people's lives; second, because modern states are expensive, they need to be able to extract resources, usually but not always through mechanisms of taxation; third, modern states seek to justify their existence, to convince the wider population of the state's essential role and of the necessity of its citizens' support.

We must acknowledge the human costs. For most Western

countries, these processes were already established by the nine-teenth century and we no longer recall either their duration or much of their substance. But the very attempt to construct modern states not only involves considerable violence (in the broad sense of coercion), but is likely also to engender resistance held by those who oppose the predominant definition of progress held by the ruling elites. We need only look at the Scottish Highland Clearances, the French Revolution, or the killing of the native peoples of North America. This is even more likely to be the case in situations where state-building is extremely rapid. Bearing these considerations in mind, we can make a more careful assessment of the forms of repression and political violence that occurred in postcolonial Africa.

Almost without exception, African elites did adopt the para-phernalia of the modern European state. For all the talk about 'African values', virtually nowhere, with the possible exception of Swaziland, were there appeals to African traditions or pre-colonial forms of social and political organisation as a way of thinking about modern government. The first parliament of Ghana was an almost exact replica of British parliamentary procedure. The constitutions of many francophone West African countries were borrowed almost word for word from that of the French Fifth Republic. The public sector was structured in the same way as the West. Indeed, in many cases, much of the structure of the colonial state was retained. These 'enhanced' African states invested considerable effort in extending control over wider society. They sought to acquire control over local power centres and bring social organisations under their super-vision. Groups that had been active in the struggle against colonial rule now found themselves hobbled, shut down or absorbed into central party structures. Peasants and rural people now found themselves being 'modernised', whether by *animation rurale* (roughly dynamism) in Senegal, or campaigns against *'obscurantismo'* (roughly, primitive superstitious beliefs) in

Mozambique. Much of this, though by no means all, was linked to attempts by African states to extract more revenue from the local economy. Since these economies were overwhelmingly agricultural this meant finding ways to tax peasants and make them more productive. In pursuit of the first objective, most African governments took greater control over agricultural marketing by making themselves monopoly purchasers of peasant crops, and, in pursuit of the second, many invested in large-scale agricultural schemes or attempts to resettle the rural population. Finally, African elites attempted to legitimise their states and policies in perfectly familiar ways. 'We are all Zambians now', said Kenneth Kaunda, the country's first president. 'For the nation to live the tribe must die', concurred Samora Machel, the first president of Mozambique. There were vague gestures towards African styles, as in the epithets that leaders liked to use – Nkrumah calling himself Osagyefo (Redeemer), and Nyerere calling himself Mwalimu (Teacher). Campaigns for cultural 'authenticity' were occasionally promoted (adopting African personal names, promoting traditional culture, renaming towns and cities). But the general tenor of African state propaganda was overwhelmingly focused on the aspiration to 'modernity'. Indeed, propaganda often came close to caricatures of Western prejudice when African parties and elites denounced the 'laziness' or 'backwardness' of their populations.

So if African elites at least tried to build modern states, if not necessarily in a conventionally democratic form, what went wrong? A first and rather obvious point is that they set themselves a very difficult task in an unrealistic time frame. Social differences in Africa were deeply entrenched, usually taking an ethnic or identity form. Such differences are based on what sociologists call 'ascriptive' characteristics like skin colour, language and religious practices, which people cannot easily hide, and which are often the basis of conflict. Conflicts based on identity are often extremely difficult to prevent, and often become very resistant to compromise. There is nothing peculiarly African about such conflicts, but they are especially prevalent in Africa. The insistence of African nationalists that the old colonial territories become states, however sensible it was in some ways, meant that the task of nation state-building would be peculiarly difficult, for the simple reason that the old colonial territories, accidents of European conquest and rivalry, contained an extraordinary variety of groups and cultures. Historically, such differences have been eroded by war, which sharpens people's group identity, and by the cultivation of historical symbols and continuities (even if these are somewhat contrived). It was by such methods that British and French identities, for example, were formed in the eighteenth and nineteenth centuries. Neither of these possibilities was easily available to modern African states. International norms, the military weakness of African states, and a certain kind of residual pan-Africanism precluded open warfare, while almost no African country, except Ethiopia, has much historical continuity or identity to draw on. African nationalism was, for tactical reasons, largely anti-colonial, as anything else would have undermined the nationalist struggle. There were occasional attempts to make connections with historic symbolism (Ghana, Mali), but these were remote from most people and largely ineffective.

African rulers were aware of these issues; indeed they had been a matter of considerable debate. Virtually everywhere in Africa in the run-up to decolonisation, and for some time afterwards, politics was divided between factions who favoured a centralised state and others who favoured a regional or autonomous structure. In Nigeria, regional and ethnic identities were so well entrenched that a one-party state was never established there, though there were plenty of military regimes. But elsewhere the 'centralisers' won the battle. In this they were greatly assisted by Africa's 'friends', who persisted in indiscriminately glorifying African nationalist regimes and condemning any opposition as treachery. It is true that, in practice, many of the more astute African leaders, such as Jomo Kenyatta, Kenneth Kaunda and Félix Houphouët-Boigny, did practise various kinds of ethnic balancing behind the scenes. But the public rhetoric, and increasingly the political practice, was hostile to locality and group and concerned with rapid 'progress' and 'modernity'. With the best will in the world, and consummate political skill, mediating the tensions between localities and groups would have been difficult. But these qualities were rather lacking. The arts of mobilising against alien rulers, who could be blamed for everything, had been mastered with considerable success; the arts of compromise, of bargaining, of going slowly, much less so.

So although African elites were concerned about national unity and were aware of the sheer variety of their societies, the way they chose to strengthen the state exacerbated rather than alleviated ethnic, regional and social tensions. Not only did the one-party state come to be seen by many as a potential threat, but also many of the actions that African states took in pursuit of national unity and development also generated antagonism, which in turn African rulers tended to suppress using the centralised states they had constructed. All over Africa, states rapidly resorted to preventive detention, even prison or 're-education' camps, often run with extreme brutality. Similar methods were used by liberation movements, which often maintained prison camps where political enemies were detained or even executed.

Those who ended up in camps included those whose faith prevented them from fully acknowledging the authority of the state. Jehovah's Witnesses and Seventh Day Adventists were harassed by several African states. The ambiguities of African nationalism are sharply illustrated by the attitude of many African governments – often extremely hostile – to indigenous African religions. The refusal of the Lumpa Church to acknowledge the Zambian state was met with ruthless force; some 700 of its members were killed in 1974. Other cultural, ethnic or regional groups that were thought to impede progress were also repressed or highly constrained. The Zimbabwe government's campaign of repression in Matabeleland in the 1980s, ostensibly against tribalism and for national unity, resulted in the deaths of some 20,000 people, mostly at the hands of a Shona force called the Fifth Brigade. African states tried to coerce nomadic peoples into permanent settlements. They were often concerned to enforce what they took to be proper 'modern' codes of dress and behaviour. Even otherwise murderous states, like that of Idi Amin, seem to have found 'backwardness' offensive. Condemning the Karimojong (a group living in northern Uganda) as hopeless savages, his government attempted to force them to give up their traditional attire and substitute Western clothing. In an incident at Nawaikorot in 1971, some 200 people appear to have been killed as part of this campaign. An extreme case perhaps, but everywhere less Westernised groups, like the Maasai in Kenya and Tanzania, were vilified for not being 'modern'. Though nothing like as vicious as Amin, the Tanzanian government for some years pursued the bizarrely named 'Operation Dress Up', designed to force Maasai people to abandon their customs and especially their mode of dress. It was also in Tanzania that the government, disappointed with the response to its calls for *Ujamaa*, a programme of villagisation, increasingly coerced the peasantry into collective villages at the point of a gun. Many African governments also have a history of hostility to people in the 'informal' economy, who were often viewed as idlers if not criminals. In 1983, the Mozambican government launched 'Operation Production', rounding up as many as 50,000 people and taking them to the countryside to build cities in the bush.

The effects of political violence and repression in postcolonial Africa, even if prompted by a desire to build effective states, more often than not had the opposite effect, provoking resistance ranging from sullen acquiescence to active, sometimes armed, opposition. The Tanzanian peasants produced less, and *Ujamaa* collapsed. The victims of Operation Production built nothing in the bush and drifted back to town. Ndebele 'tribalism' was strengthened, rather than weakened, by repression. Given time, and at least steady economic improvement, such difficulties might have been overcome. But African elites were to have neither of these, and as political struggles in Africa became more vicious, and as rulers and elites encountered increasing opposition, state-building lost any connection with an idea of the public interest and became little more than the defence of group or ethnic privilege.

Many, if not most, African leaders had developed highly centralised regimes. But leaders surrounded themselves with a small group of associates, usually from their own ethnic group, their region of origin, or even their home village. This group then monopolised all the major state offices, particularly those involving control of the armed forces and the police. In Cameroon, the first president, Ahidjo, a Fulbe, promoted other members of the Fulbe group, many from his home town of Garoua, who came to be known as the 'Garoua barons'. When he was replaced by President Paul Biya, a Christian Beti from the south of the country, public offices were increasingly monopolised by 'Beti barons'. Jomo Kenyatta's circle was from his own ethnic Kikuyu group, many of them hailing from his home district of Kiambu. By 1971, every key government department was held by Kikuyu, and Kenyatta also removed rival Kambas from senior positions in the armed forces. In Sierra Leone, President Momoh surrounded himself with fellow Limbas from his home village (known as the 'Ekutay mafia'). As these regimes became embattled they did not hesitate to harass, detain or murder their perceived opponents. In Ghana, Nkrumah introduced detention without trial, supposedly to be used only in emergencies, but increasingly used to silence political opponents. The best-known Ghanaian opposition politician, J.B. Danquah, a sick man, died in jail. Nkrumah took powers to rule by decree and to dismiss any member of the public service. In Kenya, prominent political figures like Tom Mboya, J.M. Kariuki and Robert Ouko disappeared or were murdered in suspicious circumstances that suggested the involvement of the Kenyan government. In Malawi in 1983, three cabinet ministers and an MP were beaten to death by police, though they were recorded as having died in a car crash. Repeated purges in Guinea ensured that, by the late 1970s, the regime was almost entirely drawn from the Malinke population (about a third of the country), and the inner circle mostly consisted of President Ahmed Sékou Touré's own relatives. By the time of his death in 1984, some 50,000 of his Guinean citizens had been killed, many in the notorious Camp Boiro.

This kind of murderous 'palace politics' tended to encourage the intervention of the military. In the two decades or so after independence there were some forty successful military coups and over a hundred unsuccessful ones. More often than not, these military interventions proved quite popular with African peoples because the regimes being ousted had become both repressive and corrupt. Military governments often set up enquiries into previous regimes which documented many of these behaviours. They promised to rapidly implement reforms and restore a degree of popular participation in government. In some interesting cases something like this did happen. Murtala Muhammad in Nigeria, Thomas Sankara in Burkina Faso and Jerry Rawlings in Ghana all possessed high levels of integrity and embarked on dramatic programmes of reform. But Muhammad and Sankara both made enemies and were assassinated before such reforms could gain momentum. And while they promised to reform government, the vast majority of military regimes collapsed into the same feuding that had characterised civilian regimes. African armies were rarely unified forces with a clear command structure; they were either dominated by one ethnic group or were uneasy coalitions that could easily disintegrate along the fault lines of identity.

'WE ARE TRYING TO TAKE THE MASAI FROM THE STONE AGE TO THE ATOMIC AGE'*

If one half of the burden of guilt allowed the rest of the world to indulge African states on the grounds of past injustice, the other half allowed it to indulge African states on the grounds of future achievement. This was never simply a matter of state-craft or Cold War dynamics. Why would Oxfam, committed to development and welfare, loyally cooperate with a Tanzanian government which engaged in forced migration and had more political prisoners than South Africa? The reason was sharply formulated by Tanzania's president, Julius Nyerere, who appar-ently spoke for many (doubtless including Oxfam) when he called the struggle for development 'a very real war'.

To make sense of this war, as with the one-party state, it is important to remind ourselves of details that have tended to be elided in many accounts of independent Africa. Some thirty years after independence, Africa had some of the most unequal societies in the world (indeed it still does). Moreover, the many promises of economic transformation conspicuously failed to bear fruit. How was it possible that governments led by people who had fought against the exploitation and deprivation of colonialism had achieved so little, and in many cases even seemed to have become indifferent to conditions that were some-times worse than they had been in colonial times? It is understandable that many agreed with the Nigerian sociologist, Claude Ake, when he famously commented: 'The problem is not so much that development has failed as that it was never

---

* *Nationalist*, 6 April 1968.

really on the agenda in the first place.' The despair expressed in Ake's 1996 remark was genuine and his purpose was to draw attention to the political conditions of development. But it is not, I think, quite right in that it obscures, even denies, the ways in which African states and elites did in fact pursue development.

Let's look again at the 'one-party state'. One of its major rationales was the overwhelming imperative of 'development', the pressing need in the short term to improve health, education and so on, and in the medium term to provide the resources to finance such improvements. In the longer term, Africa's leaders had to transform their economies by way of increases in agricultural efficiency and industrialisation. And all of these things had to be done in a hurry.

Much of African leaders' understanding of these issues stemmed from the resentment of colonialism and a conviction that they could do much better than colonial rulers had done. As we shall see, resentment and conviction are nowhere near sufficient, but the rationale was not in itself foolish – indeed it was generally accepted as common wisdom. Nor was there much dissent from the idea (at least until the early 1980s) that rapid growth required the intervention of a strong state and some degree of economic planning. African states became independent at a time when, in most Western countries, the state directly controlled a major part of the domestic economy and heavily influenced the rest. It would have been odd if they had radically departed from the received wisdom. There was a general consensus that the continent lacked an indigenous business class which could drive forward economic activity, and that the state bequeathed by colonialism was intended for repression and exploitation and therefore lacked the ability to plan economic development.

African leaders found these ideas congenial, as was evident in the massive proliferation of new laws, policies and public (or 'parastatal') institutions designed to promote economic development and foster national unity. New regulations were designed to control investment, trade and prices, to influence land usage, and to provide financial incentives to foreign and domestic investors. It is important to note that much of this activity cannot easily be pigeonholed as either 'economic' or 'political', or promoting either 'economic' or 'social' change. 'Indigenisation' policies, for example, which gave citizens preferential access to jobs and assets in the domestic economy either by securing certain sectors (e.g. retail, small-scale transport) for their exclusive participation or requiring foreign investors to encourage African share ownership, had two purposes. They were intended both to encourage growth by creating an African entrepreneurial class, as well as to correct the racial injustices of the past that had excluded Africans from certain fields of economic activity. Similarly, 'Africanisation' policies were intended to correct the prejudices of the colonial era and ensure that Africans had the right to pursue any career in the public service. Uniform pricing policies, and the location of large-scale projects in different parts of the country, were designed to encourage national feeling, partly by spreading the benefits of development. Huge numbers of new institutions were created, ranging from the small and local, such as cooperative societies, settlement schemes and village administrations, to nationwide public enterprises, marketing boards, development banks and bureaucratic agencies. Public corporations usually predominated in the financial, transport and industrial sectors. By 1966, Ghana had some fifty state corporations working in major industries such as steel, gold and fishing, as well as a national airline. A desperately poor country like Mali set up twenty-three state companies after independence. Much of this activity was concentrated in rural areas, where African states established many new institutions to facilitate control over rural communities and to put pressure on farmers to increase their output and productivity. Of course the precise form these policies took varied from country to country. In Guinea, the regime attempted to control virtually the whole economy, to the extent of forbidding private trade in agriculture; whereas in Malawi and Côte d'Ivoire, peasants were allowed a much greater degree of economic freedom. But while there were differences in the way African states implemented their policies, virtually all of them, whether they called themselves capitalist or socialist, practised some version of state-directed development. Most important of all, virtually everywhere the state consumed the lion's share of the available resources for investment.

It is never easy to trace connections between policies and outcomes. Governments everywhere claim credit for economic success when things go well, and disown responsibility when things go badly. But for the two decades after independence, these policies did not obstruct progress, and may well have contributed to it. During that period there was fairly rapid economic growth and a patchy, but significant, improvement in living standards. Between 1950 and 1975, the rate of economic growth in sub-Saharan Africa was 2.4% per head, though averaged over 1965 to 1980 it was 1.5% per head. Some countries did much better than that. Kenya managed 5% annual economic growth in the 1960s and 1970s. In roughly the same period, the GDP of Côte d'Ivoire doubled. Cameroon managed 7% growth from 1970 to 1985 (though this was partly based on the discovery of oil in 1977). Some of this growth suggested evidence of structural change in African economies, with industrial production expanding at twice the rate of economic growth up to 1973. Although much of this activity was in mining, manufacturing grew at about 7% per annum between 1960 and 1980. The areas of growth tended to be food processing, beverages, tobacco and textiles, mostly for the domestic market. In Kenya, between 1968 and 1974, industrial production was growing at about 9% per annum. Initially at least, food production kept up with population growth. Though this increase was achieved largely by extending the area under cultivation, rather than by means of technical innovation, there was greater use of irrigation, fertilisers and mechanisation.

There were welfare gains as well – some quite dramatic. Infant mortality fell across the continent, and life expectancy increased from 39 in 1960, to 47 in 1979. In Tanzania it increased from 40 in 1967, to 52 in 1979; and in Kenya, over roughly the same period, from 44 to 55. The expansion of education, especially primary education, was perhaps the most impressive achievement, prompting great praise from the World Bank in 1981. Africa as a whole had 63% of children in primary schools. Some countries, like Tanzania, had achieved almost universal attendance in primary school. There was a rapid expansion of universities. And something between 100,000 and 200,000 expatriate-held posts were Africanised between 1958 and 1968.

While this period of relative success should be acknowledged it proved to be short-lived, and by the end of the 1980s virtually all African countries faced severe economic difficulties. No one doubts that external shocks played a role in this. The oil price rises in 1973 and 1981 hurt African non-oil producers. Severe droughts hit parts of Africa, impacting on agriculture – most of which is rain-fed. There were dramatic collapses in the prices of certain export commodities that Africa relied on, especially coffee and cocoa. The general figures were grim. Real GDP growth declined from about 3% in the late 1970s, to about 1% in the following decade, recovering only slightly in the 1990s. Africa's share of world trade fell from 3.1% in 1960, to 1.2% in 1995. The composition of African economic activity also stagnated or deteriorated. Between 1978 and 1985, manufacturing contribution to GDP slumped from 13.5% to 6.9%.

Individual countries experienced calamitous declines. In 1967, Tanzanian exports covered the import bill, but by 1985 they barely covered a quarter. Agriculture performed particularly badly. Per capita food production actually declined – the only place in the world where this occurred. The export of traditional commodities such as cocoa, coffee, rubber, tin, spices and tropical vegetable oils declined throughout the 1970s and 1980s. Ghana's cocoa production dropped from 560,000 tons in 1965, to 249,000 tons in 1979. Nigeria, the world's largest exporter of groundnuts at independence, stopped exporting them entirely. This happened at the same time as Malaysia, Indonesia and Thailand increased their market shares for the same exports. Welfare indicators fared no better. All over Africa the achievements of the first two decades of independence at best stagnated, in many cases declined. As Africa's population continued to grow fast throughout this period, average real income per head barely increased between 1960 and 2000. Many of the standard health indicators – infant and maternal mortality, for example – stagnated, even regressed, by the 1990s. While many more children were in school, the quality of education they received was often poor, taking place in badly equipped facilities.

African states tried to buy their way out of what seemed to be temporary trouble. The global economy was flush with funds, so it was relatively easy for them to borrow on international money markets; indeed, they were encouraged to do so. However, as their fundamental economic conditions failed to improve, these debts became more and more onerous and, in the end, unsustainable.

GREED NOT GROWTH

So why then did early, if modest, successes give way to calamitous failure? Powerful currents of opinion have repeatedly insisted that the causes lie everywhere but in Africa itself. The same arguments that had been used to justify state-led development could be used to explain its lack of success. One school of thought blamed the economic aspects of the colonial legacy.

Europe had, in effect, 'underdeveloped' Africa – had damaged its economic potential so badly that recovery and further progress were bound to be extremely difficult. Another version of this argument suggested that the old colonial powers, particularly France, imposed agreements on their ex-colonies that blocked their economic progress. Some suggested that the leaders of independent Africa were little more than the puppets of 'international capital', middlemen for foreign interests concerned with nothing beyond taking their cut. Yet another school of thought looked not so much to historical factors as to the nature of the world economy, arguing that the very structure of relations between developed countries selling manufactured goods to less-developed countries selling raw materials stacked the cards against the developing world, and Africa in particular.

Some of these arguments should not be simply dismissed. It was true that, to a very large extent, colonial economies were mono-economies producing raw materials for export. The old colonial powers did, on occasion, drive very hard bargains, and the markets for raw materials experience greater price volatility and declining terms of trade, though it is also true that the terms of trade sometimes move in Africa's favour. But the deeper truth that all these arguments ignore is that all non-industrial economies have faced these difficulties. They applied as much to Australia and New Zealand in the nineteenth century as to the developing countries of South-East Asia in the twentieth. So while there is room for disagreement about exactly how we might weight the detailed causes of Africa's lack of economic progress, what seems indisputable is that arguments blaming everything on external factors make light of, even wilfully ignore, two central issues. First, there are huge challenges, both internal and external, involved in transforming relatively undeveloped economies into modern ones. But the second and more immediate issue concerns the political factors shaping African development strategies, which help to explain why they ended so badly.

The goals of many African governments were extraordinarily ambitious, in part of course driven by the rhetoric of nationalism and aspirations to 'modernity'. Kwame Nkrumah talked about 'jet-propelled' social change. The government of Mozambique imagined it could industrialise the country in ten years. President Léopold Sédar Senghor of Senegal predicted in 1969 that by 2000, the country would have tripled its per capita income. Even as slogans, African elites' understanding of development tended to focus on what was missing and how it could be acquired, rather than what Africans already had and how it could be improved. They were also vague about how such large aspirations could be rendered into concrete plans. They greatly underestimated the difficulties of rapid economic change, particularly in a continent of enormous distances and often harsh natural environments. For many members of the new elites, the 'bush' was something to escape from, not to understand or cultivate. Very few had much experience of management or economic matters. Countries that looked to the Soviet bloc for inspiration were awed by its achievements, but understood little of how they were accomplished. Leaders tended to be indifferent, sometimes actively hostile to local businesses, especially if there was a substantial 'foreign' presence like the Asian population in East Africa. Even indigenisation policies were more to do with racial justice than the active encouragement of a local entrepreneurial class.

Not surprisingly, leaders' preferences leaned towards state control and regulation. One consequence of this was a massive expansion of public employment. Rates of growth in state employment were 15% a year for Ghana and Tanzania from the 1960s to the 1980s. In Cameroon, the civil service doubled in size within six years of the accession of President Paul Biya. One estimate was that, by 1980, the public sector in Africa as a whole accounted for half of the workforce not engaged in agriculture. So African governments placed huge burdens of management on a rapidly expanding bureaucratic class, many of whose members were hugely underqualified. There was a widespread loss of competence, increasing failures of coordination between different agencies, and a general deterioration of administrative practices. And there were many other difficulties. Any kind of planning needs detailed statistical information of a kind that was lacking in most African countries where, aside from anything else, much economic activity took place outside the formal economy. Plans were drawn up by planning departments but then ignored by finance ministries and other departments. As bureaucracies mushroomed, the earlier commitment to progress and change was diluted. Kwame Nkrumah himself admitted, after his fall from power, that many civil servants had no commitment to, or understanding of, state policy. Julius Nyerere said much the same thing in 1977 – that management was preoccupied with privilege and displayed little commitment to the goals of public policy.

These general features of economic policy and management had huge consequences in both the agricultural and industrial sectors. For some time after independence, agriculture had employed up to 80% of the population and was the basis of virtually all African economies. The commitment of African elites to both development and cheap food for urban populations meant that the sector was seen as the main source of 'surplus', little more than a cash cow for the dreams of African elites. The means to extract this surplus were borrowed from colonial times. Marketing boards had often been monopoly purchasers of certain crops, partly with a view to ironing out price fluctuations but also as a way of generating revenue for the colonial state. However exploitative this might have been in colonial times, in postcolonial times these practices were actually used even more ruthlessly. In colonial Gold Coast, the state's share of cocoa sales revenue in 1947 was 3%; in independent Ghana, by 1978, it was 60%. Under pressure to pursue various objectives, states continually reduced the payments they made to peasant farmers.

Such burdens would perhaps have been manageable if there had been sufficient investment in the agricultural sector, but this was not the case. In most African countries agriculture, which accounted for 30–80% of domestic output, received less than 10% of public investment. Ghana's Seven-Year Plan (launched in 1964) contained not a single word about cocoa, the mainstay of the country's economy and the main source of public revenue! Where investment was directed into agriculture, it went to 'modern' agriculture. 'Socialist' agriculture led to state farms, even though the record of collective agriculture everywhere has been a disaster. In Ghana, the 105 state farms produced a fifth of what peasant producers could manage left to their own devices. In Mozambique they produced less than they cost. Tractors were imported at great expense, but were often inappropriate and required expensive maintenance. The things that African farmers did need – extension services, small-scale credit, regular payments for produce – were often not available or could not be sustained as economic conditions deteriorated. In these circumstances, it was not surprising that farmers voted with their feet. Crops were smuggled across borders for a better price. As much as half of Ghana's cocoa crop was smuggled into Côte d'Ivoire and Togo in the early 1980s. Alternatively, farmers simply produced less or switched to food crops. In any case, as African economies ground to a halt, there was very little for peasant farmers to buy with their income, which undermined the incentive to produce.

As agriculture was the basis of virtually every African economy, its poor performance was bound to have profound knock-on effects. For even rudimentary industrialisation to take place, African economies had to generate foreign exchange, and that meant expanding exports. This is roughly what happened in the first two decades of independence. The idea was to pursue 'import substitution industrialisation', developing enterprises behind tariff barriers and with subsidies until they could compete first in the domestic market, and then eventually export. There is nothing wrong with this in principle, but in practice it failed to take off. African governments tended to invest in 'off-the-shelf' projects that favoured foreign partners who would bring their own investment, management expertise, and technical know-how. Many of the industrial projects they invested in were not viable, and after some initial successes manufacturing petered out. Little attempt was made to connect these enterprises to the rest of the economy. Foreign firms had little incentive to explore such possibilities. For instance, a Tanzanian fertiliser factory imported all the chemicals it needed though there were domestic sources of phosphates. Many other enterprises relied on expensive imports of raw materials and spare parts, and their difficulties intensified with shortages of foreign exchange. Governments resorted to increasing subsidies to keep businesses afloat in the short term, which meant that enterprises were protected against competition without making any efficiency gains. African states made little attempt to ensure that foreign firms had incentives to ensure profitability. As a result, state enterprises operated well below their capacity (about 20% in Ghana, for example).

In the economic sphere, as in the political, many of the measures that most African states implemented could be justified as essential steps on the road to development. When those measures turned sour and failed to bear fruit, the very same measures had disastrous consequences. As the promises of African nationalism failed to materialise, and the sheer difficulties of rapid economic transformation became all too apparent, rationales quickly turned into rationalisations. The privileges of the political elite, not in themselves incompatible with a public interest in growth and development, became little more than unearned perks of office. The enormous apparatus of regulation became little more than a pool of 'rents', a means for officials to enrich themselves. The huge state sectors, far from being an engine of economic dynamism, now became a way of featherbedding the political elite, who could place close associates, or their political opponents, in lucrative positions in the economy. Ministers provided jobs to their networks and forced state banks to lend them money which would often never be repaid. Indigenisation policies, far from producing a productive entrepreneurial class, led some to funnel assets to their families or political allies, or facilitate kick-backs from foreign firms. Marketing boards, ostensibly providing price stability for peasant producers and investing in agriculture, sometimes became a form of stealth taxation and a source of loans for the well connected. State firms became vested interests determined to resist changes that threatened their positions. The 'developmental state' rapidly turned into its opposite. Any kind of policy planning became increasingly difficult. Corruption became pervasive at every level, flagrant and bloated at the elite level, but nonetheless present everywhere, making it virtually impossible for ordinary people to rely on any kind of service from the state.

In societies so ethnically and regionally divided, the consequences of politicising economic resources were disastrous. One of the reasons that African politics became so vicious so quickly was because political power became the only gateway to economic well-being. The African elites who assumed power on independence, like elites everywhere else, were not selfless or unworldly. They enjoyed the fruits of power and privilege. But they were also moved by a vision that would see their countrymen lifted from the depths of poverty and exclusion to full participation in modernity. The path to that vision rested in unity, strong states and productive economies. But the enormity of the task, the extent of their ambition and the haste with which it was pursued meant that the results could never live up to the dream. Among their citizens they encountered anxiety, resentment, instability – even resistance. If we are to talk about colonial legacy, perhaps its worst effect was that Europeans had left behind much of the appearance of a state (territorial borders, a capital), but little of the sociological reality. The new elites promised much; they claimed the exclusive right to fulfil that promise and the credit for its achievement. As hope evaporated, it would become hard to avoid taking the blame. Rulers, their circles of associates and their ethnic groups lost sight of public interest and settled for a ruthless determination to hang on to what they had acquired.

Thirty years of African nationalism had produced not a paradise but levels of conflict, instability and impoverishment unequalled anywhere on the planet. The outside world had not only taken a very indulgent view of this 'development' but had, in many ways, provided material support for it. That was now about to change.

4

THE PUNITIVE TURN

IN 1989, THE DRAMATIC COLLAPSE OF communism in the Soviet Union shattered the prevailing narratives in Africa, sweeping away all the exaggerated claims about the 'threat of communism' that African regimes had used to attract support from Western governments. In retrospect it is clear that, by the 1980s, if not earlier, there was not the faintest prospect of any kind of communism being established in Africa. The Soviet bloc countries had already begun to reduce their commitments to African states of 'socialist orientation' that they had hitherto supported. But the end of communism in its heartlands turned a strategic withdrawal into a rout, and almost overnight the argument that any African regime had to be supported because it was 'anti-communist' evaporated.

Whatever the practical obstacles to constructing communism in Africa in reality, African elites had found some inspiration in the example of Soviet economic growth and its associated political form, the Leninist state. The African 'one-party state' derived some of its legitimacy and credibility from the Soviet model. That model, however misunderstood, offered support to the idea that there really was a working alternative to liberal capitalism. When the Soviet model itself disappeared, it took the one-party state in Africa with it.

Another set of events that marked 1989 was the end of apartheid in South Africa, and with it the end of the Afrikaner-dominated state that had designed and sustained the apartheid system. The South African government had long played the 'anti-communism' card, presenting itself as a bulwark of Western civilisation and Western interests against its external (the Soviet bloc) and internal – the 'communist' African National Congress (ANC) – enemies. But with the fall of the Berlin Wall, this rhetoric lost all plausibility. The external enemies had vanished, and the ANC could now be acknowledged as nationalists determined to abolish a racially oppressive social and political order. So within South Africa, the disappearance of the Soviet camp opened up the possibility of a negotiated transition to some kind of post-apartheid society, a chance which sensible forces on both sides seized and achieved, even if at times the process proved violent and difficult.

A HOPELESS CONTINENT

Although the fall of the Berlin Wall was the more significant event globally, it was the end of apartheid that was most significant for Africa. The issue of apartheid had mobilised – almost monopolised – immense moral energy around the world. It had prompted unprecedented levels of international activity, including the first ever UN arms embargo and the promotion of economic sanctions by states and private organisations, driven by popular campaigns. The concurrent ending of both apartheid and the Cold War encouraged a widespread optimism that many international issues and problems could now be resolved. President H.W. Bush, echoed by many other Western leaders, spoke of a 'New World Order'. The moral energy mobilised in the campaigns against apartheid lost its focus, yet it did not simply fade away. People had campaigned in the belief that a racially oppressive society not only undermined the dignity of people but also severely limited their opportunities and, at its worst, condemned them to lives of poverty and deprivation. So it is not surprising that much of that moral energy came to focus instead on poverty and development. But such a redirection of energy and attention could not be limited to South Africa alone. Rather it was bound to extend its gaze to the continent as a whole. This would have huge repercussions. While most African states had supported the struggle against apartheid (and some had suffered considerable loss in doing so), the issue had also provided something of a shield behind which many African states could hide their own failings. With the end of apartheid, African states and elites found themselves exposed to an unprecedented scrutiny of their domestic records.

As we have seen in previous chapters there was indeed a great deal to scrutinise, much of it not pretty – widespread state violence and massacres, the assassination and torture of political opponents, the forced removal of whole peoples, famine and desperate poverty, massive corruption, prodigious waste of resources, mismanagement and incompetence. Ethiopia, Somalia, Sudan, Uganda, Liberia, Sierra Leone and Nigeria had experienced, or were still going through, highly destructive wars. Many more countries were politically unstable. What made this state of affairs all the more painful to contemplate was that nothing seemed to have been gained: arguably life in some parts of Africa was worse than it had been in colonial times. And it was impossible to ignore the fact that other parts of the developing world, facing similar economic and political challenges, had seen real economic progress and poverty reduction. In Africa, by the early 1990s, there had been comparatively little progress in the thirty years after independence, and this impression contributed to an atmosphere of

'Afro-pessimism'. By the end of that decade, *The Economist* could run a front cover calling Africa 'The hopeless continent'.

A greater awareness of the facts of Africa's experience since independence, and a greater readiness to face up to them, might have prompted a more hard-headed, sober assessment of the difficulties that African countries faced, and the ways they had gone about dealing with them. Thirty years on from the antagonism of colonial rule, the world had concrete experience of attempts at rapid development. What were the realistic compromises (say between agriculture and industry)? What were the priorities (say between growth and welfare, or between primary and secondary education)? How fast could these states be expected to grow? Which social changes should take priority? Why had some countries been able to develop more than African ones? It is not that these questions were never considered, but when they were it was rarely in the spirit of realism that was required. There was, after all, a vast amount of accumulated knowledge about how the now developed world made the transition to high-production, politically stable states which could have prompted useful reflection on the pace and scale of social change. The obsessive concern to explain everything by reference to colonialism, and to apportion everything in morally loaded categories of 'blame', could have been set aside in favour of more hard-headed assessments of economic and political forces and possibilities. But it did not happen; the opportunity was lost.

As on the eve of independence, everything turned on African nationalism, which had provided both the salve and the solution to the bad faith of the colonial project. But it was precisely African nationalism that was now seen to have spectacularly failed. By the 1990s, the African nationalist project lay in ruins and its champions were revealed, at best as fantasists, at worst as criminally negligent. Not only had they failed, they had bitten the hand that fed them. In the eyes of the West, African nationalism was not just a failure, but a betrayal.

HURT AND ANGER

The shock of betrayal is often followed by bitterness, anger and even rejection. So the language surrounding African states and their leaders turned from indulgent to critical, even aggressive. Western states no longer offered their African counterparts the usual courtesies that states have extended since the eighteenth century, courtesies they found it possible to maintain with plenty of other states that on occasion massacred their own people or wasted their resources. Diplomats no longer practised diplomacy but openly attacked many African leaders, denouncing them as criminals and often ostentatiously supporting their domestic opponents. Much of this rhetoric was a venting of anger, an emotional catharsis, rather than an attempt to explain anything. But just as much of the original romanticisation of African nationalism originated in academic writing, so also much of the new critical account of African states was devised in academia and taken up by others. There were two driving forces here, and while many of their practitioners did not see eye to eye, they ended up pushing in the same direction. Scholars whose primary interest was politics began to see African elites as damaging, and took to explaining why that was so. Although there were considerable differences of emphasis, a cluster of themes emerged that became known as 'neopatrimonialism'. This school of thought suggested that the main problem with African states was the absence of effective political representation of, and participation by, the mass population. Instead, African states were only linked to wider society through 'clientelist' politics, informal networks grouped around a 'Big Man' who dispensed resources in return for support. This form of politics encourages a ruthless 'zero sum' struggle for power and state resources, making it virtually impossible to formulate any sense of the 'public interest', and extremely difficult for the population to hold their leaders to account. In this new perspective, far from

African elites committing themselves body and soul to the 'development' of their societies and peoples, they now appeared grasping and venal, almost like organised criminals in their ruthless pursuit of personal enrichment.

'Neoclassical' economists, by contrast, were much less interested in the detail of African politics, but their arguments pointed in the same direction, especially in relation to the public sector. They argued that development had never been tried, and that the emphasis on the state only appealed to African elites because it opened up avenues to self-enrichment. Clientelism thrives on corruption and arbitrariness, and the scope for all these is increased by state intervention in the economy because officials can use the powers attached to their posts to enrich themselves, rather than pursue the public interest. On this analysis, economic planning by African states, far from being an effort to overcome the 'colonial legacy', mobilise economic resources, or focus effort on particular economic problems, was actually concerned with creating opportunities for politicians and civil servants to enrich themselves.

These arguments have contributed to a considerably improved account of post-independence Africa. 'Patron-clientelism', 'Big Man' politics and 'neopatrimonialism' are significant features of African politics, which does have tendencies towards corruption and the abuse of state power. And one need not be a neoclassical economist to acknowledge that the ideas and institutions of economic planning may not be wholly appropriate in countries with limited state capacities. Indeed, once these critical perspectives became commonplace, other scholars began to produce all sorts of further supporting evidence. Historians and anthropologists began to show that African nationalism was not just a heroic and unified enterprise, nobly struggling for freedom, but also consisted of hugely diverse and fractured movements. Virtually all the African nationalist movements were divided on regional, ethnic or religious grounds, often in complex combinations of all three. While the struggle against colonial rule remained paramount, these divisions often precipitated conflict between and within nationalist organisations, including conflict about dividing the spoils of office once independence was achieved. Such considerations applied to a remarkable degree to the 'liberation movements', whose military and ideological discipline appeared to many observers to promise a new kind of regime based on ideas of 'popular power', immune to the squabbles that had plagued many African states. Even here, however, that discipline eroded, and such regimes, and their leaders, fell into the same traps.

Looking back, we can see that the new academic analysis of Africa had a number of unfortunate effects. First, the vocabulary of 'neopatrimonialism' and 'patron-clientelism' provided a uniform account of Africa's condition which obscured all sorts of differences. And, second, in the hands of less scrupulous commentators in search of an easy tag, it got turned into a rhetoric of denunciation: the air was soon filled with all sorts of new labels ('predatory states', 'lame leviathans', 'rogue states', 'shanty states', even 'vampire states'), whose purpose was to serve a political agenda, rather than to make sense of reality. So despite the best intentions of scholars, the new thinking reinforced the idea that Africa's problems were the fault of its (now) malevolent elites. But in a sense this was not surprising because this new vocabulary papered over the real disagreements about the underlying causes of these problems. Arguments still rage about whether Africa's lack of development and its political instability should be seen in a wider historical context, as a function of its place in the international economy, or as an effect of the colonial legacy. These are difficult questions to which there are no easy answers. But policymakers are almost always impatient with academic niceties, so the public effect of the new realism was to reinforce pessimism and demands for new kinds of action.

So the combination of rather simplified analysis, often

amounting to little more than slogans, and the anger left by the abandonment of an overly rosy view of African nationalism, produced a demonisation of African nationalism and African leaders. If African states had previously been seen as the charges of the West, in need of our nurturing and protection, they were now denounced as devils. But who, after all, was to blame? Who should one strike out at? Much of the guilt burden story remained in place, indeed in some ways became even more naive. 'The people' must be good, their progress hampered only by the legacy of racism, slavery and colonialism. So the fault must lie with the 'bad men' at the top. The tacit bargain of decolonisation had been that African elites would complete the business of development and modernisation. That business could no longer, it now seemed, be entrusted to those elites. The tasks of modernisation, so badly neglected in the colonial period, and taken insufficiently seriously in the post-independence period, must now be resumed. Africa's development became international 'unfinished business'.

It followed that the relation between Africa's leaders and the tasks of modernisation had to be invested with new energy. It would not be enough to denounce, demonise, and discredit these elites. Ways had to be found to bring pressure to bear on them, or even to circumvent them. African leaders, having been the solution, now became the problem. But how could this problem be solved? Such leaders represented sovereign states, entitled in principle to all the respect and privileges that for some 150 years sovereign states have accorded each other, inscribed in the traditions of diplomacy. The whole point about decolonisation was that it could not be a half-way house, that nothing less than full sovereignty would do. African territories had after all demanded nothing more for themselves than the western powers had long insisted was their own historical right. A return to colonialism was unthinkable, but some way had to be found to constrain the sovereignty of states The pursuit of this goal heralded a remarkable revival of what can only be called quasi-colonial modes of thinking.

A NEW 'STANDARD OF CIVILISATION'?

It is commonplace, as we noted in chapter 1, to caricature colonial rule as mere brutality and exploitation, nothing less than a 'crime against humanity', and to condemn those who defend it as liars or racists. But in the early nineteenth century, Africa's perceived backwardness was usually explained by the effects of the slave trade. It was widely thought that the trade, as well as being morally wrong, stimulated slave raiding, war between African societies, and general disorder and destruction. Ending the slave trade would not only bring an end to this disorder but also make possible the development of Africa through 'legitimate commerce'.

A great deal hung on this idea, and attempts were made in the mid-nineteenth century to develop such commerce, especially in the export of oils to supply growing industrial and food markets in Europe. However, this commerce was not only seen to have failed but also, in a cruel paradox, to have renewed slavery within Africa. In some African societies, men of power and influence, now deprived of Atlantic slave markets, turned to local slave labour to produce goods for Western consumption. This wholly unforeseen development prompted the idea that it was not enough to abolish the trade outside Africa; the trade within the continent must be abolished as well. These sentiments, though they did not on their own cause the 'scramble for Africa' of the late nineteenth century, were undoubtedly a major element in the widespread support for the colonial idea. Africa's problems would be largely solved by peace and trade, and the obstacles to both of these, such as slavers, would be suppressed by colonial rule. So the idea that the main obstacle to progress in Africa is malign elites is not new.

What made all this even more plausible in the nineteenth and early twentieth century was that it fitted comfortably into a broader set of assumptions made by the 'great powers', known then as the 'standard of civilisation'. This doctrine viewed the world as a series of concentric circles. The first was an inner circle of civilised, Christian, European 'great powers' abiding by shared norms of conduct and behaviour. A second circle comprised powers that were close to the first, or were going to join it in the near future (the United States, Japan, some Latin American countries). A third circle consisted of countries that, while they remained distinct states, were generally seen to be problematic in terms of their internal social structures (China, Turkey, Egypt), even if they had once been great powers in their own right. Ottoman Turkey, for example, was known in the nineteenth century as the 'sick man of Europe'. Outside these circles the rest of the world's societies were thought to be so far behind the civilised world as to be likely to remain 'backward' for the foreseeable future.

What followed from this picture were three crucial principles. First, the sovereignty of states was a matter of degree, dependent on how 'civilised' they were. Only civilised states were fully sovereign, while less civilised states might have limited degrees of sovereignty. Second, it was assumed that fully sovereign states could legitimately exert control over partially sovereign states, though precisely what form that might take varied from case to case. In nineteenth-century China, for example, several European powers 'leased' territory, intervened in Chinese politics, and imposed unequal treaties on the country, but it remained in some sense an independent state. The British and French ambassadors to Ottoman Turkey in the nineteenth century were far more than ambassadors; they exerted real pressure on Turkey's rulers across a whole range of internal matters. But over large parts of the world – the Indian subcontinent, South-East Asia, and virtually all of Africa – powerful states exercised direct control in the form of colonial rule.

The third, and really crucial point as far as the contemporary revival of these ideas is concerned, was that intervention by civilised states in the affairs of less civilised states was permissible, not simply in the pursuit of self-interest, but in order to improve the internal conditions of such states. Indeed, it was often argued, as the idea of 'legitimate commerce' suggests, that the pursuit of self-interest and the betterment of others were complementary. For example, broadly speaking the colonial powers in Africa said they were going to suppress the slave trade, and they did. So although often vitiated by bad faith, such notions became a part of state practice. They were, for example, inscribed into the League of Nations Charter after the First World War. The formula in that document gives a flavour of the idea:

> To those colonies and territories which as a consequence of the late war have ceased to be under the sovereignty of the States which formerly governed them and which are inhabited by peoples not yet able to stand by themselves under the strenuous conditions of the modern world, there should be applied the principle that the well-being and development of such peoples form a sacred trust of civilization and that securities for the performance of this trust should be embodied in this Covenant.

Nor should we imagine that such language was confined to states. The British Anti-Slavery Society, in its day a 'progressive' organisation, talked of the 'child races of the world'. Such language was quite common, and it is the tone and assumptions that strike modern ears as outrageous because they assume degrees of 'civilisation'. But at the time the idea was taken sufficiently seriously that the territories identified in the Charter were called mandates and came under the supervision of one of the colonial powers, which in turn were required to report to the League's Mandates Commission. When the League of

Nations was replaced by the United Nations after the Second World War, mandates were replaced by trusteeships.

The modern parallels are quite striking. There was a similar readiness to blame African elites, to manipulate those elites without completely undermining them, and also aspirations to make them do the 'right' things. But there was also a deeper intuition that more fundamental changes needed to be made in African societies to make them 'modern'. Acknowledging these similarities however, we should also be aware of the changed circumstances of the late twentieth and early twenty-first centuries. What justified diminished sovereignty for the 'standard of civilisation' was the 'backwardness' of some peoples. Such an argument is not available to modern states, which are committed to notions of equality that exclude the possibility that people can really be different. Instead, Western states now began to promote the notion of human rights. In this new understanding, properly sovereign states are those that observe the human rights of their populations. Sovereignty is not now a matter of degree but a binary: states that do not respect human rights are not properly sovereign and, in principle at least, may be the subject of outside intervention. But there is a second important difference between then and now. In the standard of civilisation argument, the more or less self-evident fact of 'backwardness' warranted using force to advance civilised standards. But the whole idea of compulsion of a colonial kind has become unthinkable. There is thus a tension between a modern strain of thought that rejects assumptions about 'backwardness' and cultural superiority, and refuses the colonial idea of rule or trusteeship, but nonetheless, through the idea of 'human rights', attempts to revive the 'standard of civilisation', weaken the sovereignty of some countries, and authorise engagement with their domestic societies.

Other political circumstances have also changed since colonial times. Sovereignty is embedded in the international order, and states are extremely reluctant to see it infringed in practice, even if they are prepared to concede the possibility in theory. Even though the 'great powers' still exercise huge influence in the world, international relations are much more multilateral, and agreements have to be secured rather than assumed. Such tensions are never finally resolved in politics or international relations, but they constantly surface both theoretically and in the policy arena. The effect of these changes was to create a shallow consensus around a loose agenda, but much argument and debate about the details.

The endemic conflicts of African politics would have to end, as these were plainly incompatible with development. To make this happen, the West would have to abandon its constraints on intervention in domestic conflicts. An inevitable consequence of this was the beginning of the 'criminalisation' of African politics, which came to be seen as a struggle between 'good' and 'bad' actors. This suggested that, if methods could be found to remove the bad actors, they should be used. This was novel territory. There were huge unanswered questions as to who should intervene, on what grounds, and for how long. But those were precisely the issues that the major powers began to explore.

PUNISHING ELITES

A number of developments in international politics gave this process momentum. First, major states began to apply sanctions against countries whose social and political practices they considered unacceptable. Sanctions might mean general threats, such as the suspension of aid packages, or they might be targeted against specific leaders of recalcitrant regimes. Indeed, the 1990s came to be known as the 'sanctions decade'. Western states were also prepared to contemplate tougher action against countries like Iraq and Serbia without much fear of retaliation. In these two cases such action ran the full gamut, from destructive sanctions to intensive bombardment, and ultimately military invasion and occupation. Although all these new developments were largely driven by individual states, they signalled a trend towards multilateralism. But since the major Western powers more or less shared the same views, they often found it more convenient to act through international organisations which they largely controlled. Between 1945 and 1990, the UN Security Council had imposed sanctions only twice (against South Africa and Rhodesia). In the 1990s it imposed them sixteen times. But there was little objection as these international organisations were keen to develop their influence, and sanctions were vociferously supported by various NGOs. Historically, such groups had largely avoided overtly 'political' stands, particularly on international issues, but from the end of the Cold War they increasingly presented themselves as part of 'global civil society', despite the fact they were not accountable to anyone.

It did not take long for these new weapons to be used against African countries. Western states took the lead in this area, having little fear of retaliation. Arms embargoes were imposed on Angola, Côte d'Ivoire, the Democratic Republic of the Congo (DRC), Ethiopia, Eritrea, Liberia, Libya, Rwanda, Sierra Leone and Somalia. New kinds of commodity embargoes were developed on diamond exports from Angola, Sierra Leone, Liberia and Côte d'Ivoire; timber exports from Liberia; and charcoal exports from Somalia. But by the end of the 'sanctions decade', the West began to believe that sanctions were too blunt a weapon. Instead, they developed 'smart sanctions'. The British, Swiss and German governments all funded conferences in which various academic experts were recruited to devise them. 'Smart sanctions' came to be targeted more and more at individuals and leaders of states, or military/political movements. The European Union took the lead in applying such sanctions and refining their use. But however 'smart' the practice of sanctions, it remained open to accusations of bias. The vast majority of smart sanctions, excluding terrorism cases, have been carried out against Africans. The lists of people banned or restricted were often arbitrary or out of date. Targets could claim that basic legal principles were breached, that they were unaware of the charges against them, or that the evidence for the charges was not open to scrutiny, and it was unclear what they needed to do to have sanctions withdrawn.

More recently, Western states and certain NGOs have sought other avenues, such as legal action against African leaders in Western courts. Though judgments are often overturned by higher courts, they form part of a now persistent strategy to undermine the sovereignty of states by attacking the immunity of state officials, up to and including heads of state. The West has also funded prosecutions in African states and supported domestic organisations within African countries to scrutinise their governments and bring prosecutions in corruption cases. Although, at the moment, such proposals remain politically fanciful, the same academic experts have been devising further measures which would subject African states and their leaders to internationally controlled mechanisms. Increasingly, the 'expert' literature on this range of punitive techniques sees them as an integrated toolkit to be deployed against particular targets.

The inadequacy of sanctions was one of a number of factors which contributed to the establishment of an International Criminal Court (ICC) which could, in certain circumstances, override the sovereignty of states. Its rules were agreed in 1998, and, having been ratified by sixty states, it came into existence in 2002. Drawing on the precedent of the postwar Nuremberg and Tokyo trials, individuals could now be held responsible for breaches of international law by states they led or controlled. In contrast to sanctions and temporary arrangements, like the ad hoc legal tribunals in Sierra Leone and Rwanda, the ICC had all the legitimacy of 'the law' and being 'a court', and it quickly became clear that it was the perfect instrument to pursue the criminalisation of African politics.

In its fifteen-year existence, the ICC has only pursued cases against African countries. Arrest warrants against named individuals have only been issued in the DRC and Uganda (2004), Sudan (2005), Central African Republic (2007), Kenya (2010), Libya (2011), Côte d'Ivoire (2011) and Mali (2015), prompted by the International Crisis Group and Amnesty International which, along with others, have formed a coalition of NGOs vigorously promoting the ICC. With a remarkably narrow focus on Africa, these organisations have produced a constant stream of reports, which are intended to encourage new sanctions. The ICC was by no means seen as a replacement for sanctions, but rather as an additional weapon: the UN Security Council referred Sudan to the ICC in the same week it announced sanctions against the country.

The ultimate form of undermining sovereignty is, of course, military coercion. Before the Second World War the 'great powers' did not hesitate to resort to punitive expeditions to coerce weaker states, sometimes justifying such practices in terms that went beyond self-interest. After the Second World War however, with the entrenchment in international law and state practice of strong notions of sovereignty and the illegitimacy of war except in self-defence, such practices virtually disappeared. Wars still took place, but not usually over the domestic social systems of the protagonists. When they did, they were deeply unpopular, as in the Vietnam War. The revival of 'standard of civilisation' ideas, however, opened new possibilities for military intervention intended precisely to change a state's internal social structure. Because sovereignty is strongly entrenched as an international norm, and the public are often suspicious of attempts to override it, the arguments for it have to be spelt out with some care, and the political complexities of such interventions are formidable. Who is to carry out the intervention? How long should it last? Who should pay for it? What are the criteria for success? Despite these manifold difficulties, the 'great powers' have on occasion intervened in the internal affairs of states, notably African states. These interventions were inconsistent, poorly planned, and shaped by all sorts of circumstances, but they are not usefully understood to be in direct pursuit of self-interest.

The tensions in this developing agenda were apparent in the first two interventions in post-Cold War Africa. In the early 1990s, a number of Western states helped to broker a peace deal in Mozambique between the government, controlled by the ruling party Frelimo, and an opposition movement, Renamo. Once there was a peace to keep, they used the United Nations to police it. There was one novelty: Renamo had demanded, and the government had conceded, multiparty elections, so the United Nations organised, paid for, and supervised a poll in 1994, which resulted in a Frelimo victory, but a respectable electoral performance by Renamo. It was peace-keeping in the old-fashioned sense. Throughout the transition to peace, the Mozambican government remained the legitimate government, and the country retained full sovereignty. There were no attempts to demonise the combatants (though both sides had committed atrocities); there were no show trials; there were no demands for 'justice'. The Mozambican government devised the electoral system and got its way, even though the 'great powers' favoured a different arrangement. Within months of the election the United Nations had withdrawn. Peace brought a massive increase in foreign aid and increasing interference in Mozambique's economic policy, but otherwise the country was pretty much left to its own devices.

The situation in Somalia, an amalgamation of a British and Italian colony which became independent in 1960, was much messier. Plagued from the beginning by political instability, military strongman General Mohamed Siad Barre seized power in 1969. Following a familiar pattern, early promises of development were undermined by environmental difficulties, economic collapse and conflict with neighbouring Ethiopia, all made much worse by Great Power meddling. In the face of increasing domestic opposition, the regime retreated into its clan and family bunker, resorting to ruthless methods of repression. Assailed by a number of armed movements, the regime finally collapsed in January 1991, descending into a vicious factional conflict.

NGOs called for intervention on humanitarian grounds, and the 'great powers' proved sympathetic. Peace was imposed, and humanitarian relief provided. But the intervention, started by the US and then placed under a UN umbrella, rapidly took on a political dimension. The US ambassador to the UN said it wanted nothing less than the restoration of an entire country. The UN clearly favoured one faction, ensuring that the situation further deteriorated to the point of open conflict between UN 'peace-keepers' and the Somali population. Soon, the political will of the 'great powers' to pursue the project was exhausted, and the UN ignominiously withdrew in 1995.[*]

Despite the failure of the intervention in Somalia, it became the model for future engagements in Africa, weaving sanctions, legal indictments and, ultimately, military intervention together. The conflict in Sierra Leone, which began in 1991, was rooted in the collapse of the country's economy, endemic poverty, extraordinary levels of corruption among the ruling elites and persistent factionalism inside the armed forces. Initially it attracted little international attention – although some support was provided to Nigeria to contain the main rebel group, the Revolutionary United Front (RUF) – while trying to negotiate some more permanent political settlement. This seemed to have been achieved in July 1999, when the RUF agreed to participate

---

[*] I discuss later developments in Somalia in chapter 7.

in government. The agreement quickly broke down, and renewed violence brought about greater involvement of the major powers and the UN. A large UN force – the United Nations Mission in Sierra Leone (UNAMSIL) – of some 6,000 military personnel (later increased to 11,000) was deployed in October 1999. In May, some 500 members of this mission were kidnapped by rebel forces, prompting appeals for help from the secretary general of the UN. Unilateral military action by Britain succeeded in reinforcing the morale of the UN operation, and the main rebel group was subsequently defeated.

Several novelties marked the intervention in Sierra Leone. First, the UN had begun to impose sanctions in 1997 on the Sierra Leone government, and later on the main rebel group, which became a more developed regime aiming to limit the sale of conflict diamonds. Second, it was marked by tension, but also complementarity between a major power and the UN. On the ground, British intervention remained under strict British command, but was in part motivated by a desire to support United Nations peace-keeping efforts. Third, it suggested that the scale of such interventions would increase. At full strength, the UN operation in Sierra Leone had comprised 18,000 members. Fourth, it took another step away from seeing conflict resolution as expediting a peace agreement between combatants – Britain and the UN were now making their own judgements about combatants and imposing peace on the 'bad' ones. This step was reinforced by the creation of a special court, justified by the relatively novel doctrine that there could be no peace without justice, and the 'bad men' must be treated as criminals.

The coordination and calibration of these techniques has become increasingly sophisticated, as the recent intervention against Côte d'Ivoire shows. This West African country had been one of Africa's success stories, but ran into difficulties in the 1980s. For some time, President Houphouët-Boigny's political skills in managing the increasing tension between the northern and southern parts of the country had kept the crisis at bay, but with his death in 1993 that crisis quickly became acute, with northern rebels engaged in periodic fighting with the government in the capital city of Abidjan. From 2003, the United Nations had deployed peace-keepers and attempted to mediate, but they proved increasingly one-sided and hostile towards the government of Laurent Gbagbo. There were forceful attacks on the Ivorian army, as well as violent repression of popular protest in the capital. Rebel groups continued to have easy access to arms, which the UN and France did little to impede. The Ivorian government repeatedly requested French troops to leave the country, requests which were simply ignored. A protracted process of negotiations produced a political settlement culminating in elections, held in 2010. But the results of these elections were disputed, and open conflict resumed.

At this point the Western powers (and some African states) turned decisively against President Gbagbo. The World Bank, the IMF and the African Development Bank stopped all credit lines for the country. The EU imposed sanctions on Gbagbo, his associates, and business organisations linked to him. This led other banks to suspend activities in the country, and these intensifying financial difficulties made it difficult for Gbagbo to secure the loyalty of his officials and troops. In March 2013, the UN Security Council opened the way to more decisive military intervention, authorising the use of force against the wishes of a functioning state – indeed, authorising any use of force, supposedly to protect civilians. In April, having seized control of Abidjan airport, ostensibly for the evacuation of foreign nationals, French and UN forces went into action against Gbagbo in the capital, bombing the presidential palace, military camps, and the Ivorian radio and television network. The public justification for this action was to prevent heavy weapons being used against civilians, but it was clear that that French and the UN were determined to install the rebel leader, Alassane Ouattara, in power. For some days the Gbagbo camp continued to resist, until UN and French forces openly attacked his remaining strongholds, firing missiles at the presidential palace and sections of Abidjan city which were pro-Gbagbo, and using tanks to overcome all resistance. The French contrived to allow rebel forces to arrest the Ivorian president via a corridor leading directly from the French Embassy to the presidential residence, and he was held for several months by the Ouatarra government before being transferred to The Hague, pending trial before the ICC.

One further case illustrates the growing ruthlessness with which such interventions can now be pursued. In early 2011, encouraged by political protests elsewhere in North Africa, there were demonstrations against Colonel Gaddafi's Libyan government, especially in the eastern regions of the country, which broadened into rebellion and were met with repression. Despite initial reluctance to intervene, the Western powers soon insisted that Gaddafi had to renounce power. First the EU, then the UN, mandated sanctions (asset seizures and travel bans) against him and other officials. The UN referred the situation in Libya to the ICC (only the second such referral, the other being Sudan in 2005). In March, a no-fly zone was ordered by the UN Security Council. These measures were ostensibly taken to avoid massacres of civilians by the regime, but it rapidly became clear that the real purpose of these activities was regime change, as NATO forces now engaged in direct attacks on government forces and, abandoning any pretence of neutrality, supplied considerable military and other support, including training and special forces, to insurgent groups. The regime duly collapsed, and Gaddafi was killed in October.*

The parallels, as well as the differences, between the Ivorian and Libyan cases are intriguing. They shared an increasing use

---

* Since then, the situation in Libya has remained chaotic – a point to which I will return in chapter 7.

of, and coordination between, punitive instruments of sanctions, judicial procedures and military coercion. The 'peace-keepers' criminalised one party and promoted the other. Their rationales tend to be constrained at first, but then more and more openly veered towards 'regime change'. (Differences remain. In some cases, one major power takes the lead, dragging others along. The US was a reluctant supporter of the intervention in Libya which was driven forward by the UK and France. There are practical considerations as well. It is much easier to pursue such intervention in countries with coastlines, where airpower can be decisive.)

As these two recent cases show, interventions have become more intrusive and more extensive – what their promoters would call 'robust'. They have even spawned their own vocabulary: terms such as 'peace enforcement', 'peace-building' and, at their most self-congratulatory, 'the liberal peace'. But the deeper the intervention, the more difficult it is to escape its consequences. Although some of the interventions I have described bear more than a passing resemblance to colonial rule, the fact is African states remain sovereign. They cannot be returned to colonial or mandate or trusteeship status. Under these circumstances, even coercive interventions – like those in Côte d'Ivoire and Libya – can only provide a breathing space. The question remains of how to deal with states that do not make the best of their sovereignty.

There are really only two possibilities. One is to set up international frameworks to which all states are subject. This has the great advantage of not appearing to single out any state or groups of states for special treatment. In practice, of course, strong states can often evade supposedly international rules where weak states generally cannot. Most African states remain weak, so 'universal' rules are more easily imposed on them. The second, much more ambitious, and much more difficult way is to change African societies from the inside. Western states might pressure leaders to take the tasks of development seriously, and the most effective way to do that is to try to mobilise certain kinds of local social forces to put pressures on those elites so that they start to behave the way they 'should'. The ways these techniques work, and their complexities and problems, will be explored in the next two chapters.

5

IMPOSING RULES

PUNITIVE MEASURES – AGGRESSIVE RHETORIC, TARGETING of individuals, sanctions against political organisations, even the deployment of armed force – are relatively easy to initiate, even without any clear political objective. But they do not in themselves produce any kind of alternative, nor any guidance as to how to revive the Western development project.

Even before the end of the Cold War, African development was clearly faltering. The first attempts to subject African states to an external agenda came in the form of economic policy. Across most of the Western capitalist world, a revived orthodoxy emerged that the best way to manage all economies was through market forces, rather than by means of planning or state direction.* This consensus quickly spread from domestic to development policy. The idea that developing countries required different policy approaches was discredited. Instead, everyone was subject to the same economic 'laws'. Any attempt to secure

---

* The standard label for this view is 'neoclassical' economics, sometimes also labelled 'neo-liberalism'.

rapid growth by means of planning and state-directed investment was therefore mistaken and should be replaced by the
'invisible hand' of the market. Certain international organisations, notably the 'Bretton Woods' institutions (BWIs) – the
collective name for the World Bank and the International
Monetary Fund – rapidly adopted the new orthodoxy, partly
for analytical reasons, but also under pressure from their major
shareholders, especially the United States and the United
Kingdom, whose new governments, under President Ronald
Reagan and Prime Minister Margaret Thatcher, were enthusiastic
proponents of the new market orthodoxy.

It must also be said that the 1980s was a disastrous decade for
Africa, as most of its economies experienced severe slowdowns or
contractions in their economic growth. They took on more debt,
thinking to tide themselves over, but this strategy failed. Between
1970 and 1976, Africa's public debt increased fourfold. By 1980 this
debt had reached $55 billion, and a decade later it stood at
$160 billion. At the same time, global interest rates increased
sharply. So African states were in no position to resist the imposition of new economic policies. By restricting these impositions,
at least initially, to the economic sphere, the major powers could
avoid the charge that they were trespassing on the sovereignty of
African states. Both the 'great powers' and the international financial institutions (IFIs) were careful to stress that they were only
insisting on demands to change economic policies of African states,
and not interfering directly in their politics.

GETTING THE PRICES RIGHT?

Thus began the period of 'structural adjustment' first outlined
in the Berg Report published in 1981.* Berg made three main

---

* *Accelerated Development in Sub-Saharan Africa: An Agenda for Action*
  (Washington, DC: World Bank, 1981).

points. First, that Africa's failure to develop was primarily due to domestic policy inadequacies. The role of external shocks and structural features of the international economy were acknowledged, but deemed to be secondary. Second, the main priority was to bring about a fundamental reorientation of economic policy towards the agricultural sector. Third, this new policy should prioritise raising producer prices to farmers, easing exchange controls, and generally allowing markets to function more freely. Although the report was controversial at the time, after much debate the World Bank accepted it and used it to shape policy. A steady stream of publications built on the report, which hardened into a doctrine that became known as the 'Washington Consensus' (the World Bank, the International Monetary Fund and the US Treasury Department are all headquartered in that city). The IMF and the World Bank approached this from rather different directions rooted in their different roles. The IMF focused on macroeconomic stability, dealing with inflation, public expenditure and trade balances (roughly what economists call 'demand-side' issues). Its focus was on stabilising economies and bringing inflation, high levels of public debt or trade imbalances under control, essentially by restraining demand. Its favourite techniques include devaluation of currency, reduction in public expenditure, and trade liberalisation. The World Bank, by contrast, was conceived as a development financing institution, enhancing the productive capacities of economies (the 'supply-side'). Until the early 1980s, this meant investment in the form of long-term concessional loans to countries to fund infrastructure (transport and energy projects). Later, the World Bank focused on advice and funding for economic management, regulations, state enterprises, competition policy and such matters. So the standard IMF package emphasised stabilisation, whereas the standard World Bank package emphasised structural adjustment.

Despite these differences, both institutions shared a common vision of market-oriented approaches to economic management which identified two imperatives. The first was to reduce state involvement in the management of economies, and the second was to ensure that the freed-up economic sphere operated according to market incentives. This meant the removal of negative state controls or limitations on economic activity, as well as the introduction of positive incentives. So states were required to let markets determine exchange rates or wage rates, and they were forbidden to use, or at least limited in their use of, subsidies. With these practices restrained, African governments were expected to reduce public expenditure and public sector employment, privatise those sectors of the economy under state control, encourage the development of capital markets, use incentives to attract foreign direct investment, and to marketise public services like health and education by means of user fees. Armed with these prescriptions, the Bretton Woods institutions became the dominant players in the development project. While the two institutions often differed on issues such as how fast reform should be implemented, their collaboration became increasingly close. In any case, most poor African countries were in no position to refuse them. This was not merely a question of the resources they commanded and the penalties they could impose, but also their global predominance. They not only commanded a large institutional weight of expertise but also increasingly played the role of gatekeepers in relation to other investors and debt holders dealing with Africa. More often than not, African states could not secure agreement from other states or commercial debt holders unless they had the Fund's and the Bank's blessing.

In the face of fairly overwhelming pressures most African states succumbed, and at some point almost all of them agreed structural adjustment policies with the BWIs. There were hundreds of agreements in total, usually following a fairly standardised template. Zambia's agreements in 1983 and 1985 included devaluation of the currency, a 5% limit on wage increases, the removal of price controls on several essential commodities and subsidies on maize and fertilisers. The country was also required to open up its foreign trade with the adoption of a foreign exchange auction system and the elimination of its import licensing system. Other measures included liberalisation of agricultural marketing, public sector reform and reductions in the civil service. In the short term, such measures (especially the removal of food subsidies) would lead to considerable economic distress and, as in Zambia, Tanzania and Sudan, protests and riots. In Zambia, authorities first tried to repress protest, but popular resistance prompted a rethink and the Zambian government repudiated its agreements with the IMF instead. It was here that the BWIs' gatekeeper role proved crucial: no other lenders would provide resources for the country, so it was forced back to the IMF and required to implement further policy changes.

Sometimes the BWIs and the donors exerted considerable pressure in order to achieve very specific goals. Despite repeated assertions that the imposition of structural adjustment policies was 'not political', the Fund and the Bank used their financial clout to demand very specific policy changes by African states that went well beyond a concern with macroeconomic imbalances. Zambia was told to privatise its copper mining, a mainstay of the economy. Continual pressure was maintained during the 1990s, and in 1999 the donors withheld a substantial amount of aid and threatened to postpone relief of the country's debt burden. The Zambian finance minister said 'we had no choice'. In Mozambique, the World Bank led demands that the export duty on cashew nuts (which was in place to ensure that they were processed in factories in Mozambique), be removed, and cashews freely exported. In the face of considerable protest, the Bank stuck to its guns and threatened to hold up the country's access to aid. The government had to give way. In 1998, the

World Bank threatened to withdraw all support for Tanzania's energy sector if it proceeded with plans for new power projects. The same government faced strong pressures from the IMF to privatise its banking system. All over Africa, the Bank and the Fund used their leverage over African governments to impose broad policy choices, such as the privatisation of water supplies and user fees for education and medical services (although both these policies were later abandoned).

WHAT ABOUT THE POLITICS?

Throughout the first decade or so of structural adjustment the BWIs resolutely maintained they were 'non-political', a requirement of their founding charters, and that their only concern was with economic 'laws'. This was true in that they did not concern themselves overtly with regimes, political parties, ideologies and so on. By the early 1990s, however, this self-denying ordinance was coming under increasing strain. A decade of structural adjustment did not seem to be having a very positive effect, certainly nothing even approximating what had been promised. There is room for genuine disagreement about this outcome – the BWIs argued that there had been some success, but many African countries were not following the appropriate policies, whereas their critics countered that the policies were misconceived, irrelevant, or even damaging. But even while continuing to defend and refine the policy, the BWIs began to believe that the political aspects of growth and development could no longer be ignored.

A number of considerations had prompted this rethink. One was that African states and their elites were increasingly learning to 'play the game', nominally accepting the conditions of structural adjustment, but doing little to implement them. They would cherry-pick the obvious and easily implemented conditions –

say, ending food subsidies – and stall on institutional changes. They would take out new loans to pay off old ones. They would claim that reforms needed more time to work. Second, the BWIs were vulnerable to the criticism, famously outlined in the 1987 UNICEF document *Adjustment with a Human Face*,* that they had ignored the social consequences of structural adjustment, particularly its impact on the poor. As a growing number of influential NGOs took up this theme, the BWIs needed to claw back some ground.

The World Development Report is the World Bank's showcase publication aimed at the wider aid and development world. Its 1990 edition was devoted to the theme of poverty. The BWIs began to believe that the reform of Africa's economies could only be achieved with the willing collaboration, rather than the enforced compliance, of Africa's political elites. The idea that everything would be solved by 'rolling back the state' and 'getting the prices right' had also come in for heavy criticism and prompted a rethink about the role of the state in economic development. A 1989 World Bank report had suggested that underlying Africa's development problems was a 'crisis of governance'.** But the BWIs on their own were in no position to abandon the 'no politics' rule. What made that possible was the end of the Cold War.

The Berlin Wall had hardly crumbled before a torrent of demands for political change in Africa began to emerge from the Western powers and international agencies. The British foreign secretary called for encouragement to countries 'which tend towards pluralism, public accountability, respect for the rule of law, human rights and market principles'; two years later his colleague added transparency, regular elections, freedom of

---

* UNICEF, *Annual Report 1987* (New York: UNICEF, 1987). Retrieved from https://www.unicef.org/about/history/files/unicef_annual_report_1987.pdf
** I will discuss 'governance' in the next chapter.

expression; a 1991 United States Agency for International Development 'Democracy and Governance Policy Paper' called for 'democratic values'. The German Ministry for Economic Cooperation reported that criteria for aid would include polit-ical participation and a responsible and accountable government. Not to be outdone, the president of France, a country not hith-erto noted for its devotion to democracy in Africa, announced in June 1990 that authoritarian states would receive less French aid than others.

International organisations rapidly responded to the changing tone. The Commonwealth countries committed themselves to a new statement of principles, the Harare Declaration, which removed a previous reference to the rejection of 'international coercion'. The European Union, revising its Lome IV treaty with its development partners in 1989, inserted a reference to human rights in the text, rather than just the preamble, and when these arrangements were further consolidated in the Maastricht Treaty in 1991 and 1995 it added a suspension clause allowing it to withhold aid from countries breaching these principles. The UN General Assembly asserted in December 1991 that periodic and genuine elections were crucial. NGOs piled on, too. Organisations which for years had bowed the knee to African states now began to notice their inadequacies. They were not slow either to argue that they were much more capable of carrying out development than African states. These weighty declarations were soon followed by action. The US suspended aid to Zaire in September 1991. In Chad, the French refused to protect Hissène Habré's regime against domestic opposition as they had done in the past. At various times in the 1990s, the EU suspended aid to Comoros, Equatorial Guinea, Gambia, Kenya, Malawi, Nigeria, Niger, Sudan, Togo and Zaire. Some African states clearly moved to anticipate these developments. In Côte d'Ivoire the govern-ment quickly legalised opposition parties, and in Benin President Mathieu Kérékou handed over power to a transitional government which convened multiparty elections. In some cases very direct pressure was exerted on countries to comply with overtly political changes. In Kenya (1991) and Malawi (1992) there was considerable coordination between donors, who suspended most kinds of aid until their demands for constitutional change had been met.

Despite occasionally rather dramatic examples, in the early stages at least political conditionalities tended to overlap with their economic counterparts, stressing participation, say, rather than democracy as such. But the general thrust was pretty clear – after all, more or less the same package was pressed on Eastern European countries after the collapse of the Soviet bloc. So, for example, following the annulment of Nigeria's 1993 election the European Union and other international bodies imposed limited sanctions on the country. The United States, United Kingdom and other countries recalled their ambassadors. The Commonwealth suspended Nigeria's membership, and both the United Nations and Organisation of African Unity condemned Nigeria for its human rights record. The EU suspended project development cooperation with Nigeria (though other kinds of aid continued). They did sometimes offer 'positive' conditionalities – resources to encourage or sustain certain kinds of political change. With the restoration of civilian rule in Nigeria in 1998, all sanctions were lifted and the aid taps were quickly turned back on.

As they were fleshed out, economic and political conditionalities became more problematic. As general principles and as political rhetoric, 'the market' and democracy might muster universal consensus, but translating them into policies opened up a host of ambiguities. Even the most enthusiastic market ideologues acknowledged there was a considerable gap between general principles and specific policies. Much the same applied to political conditionalities. Although certain general nostrums were beyond question (democracy, human rights, etc.), what these meant in practice was difficult to discern. There were, of course, genuine difficulties. Which of these issues was most important? What if one aspect improved and another did not? How to measure improvement? In practice, such difficulties were dealt with on a case-by-case basis. The BWIs were much tougher with some African countries than with others.

Between Western states, even within them, there was disagreement on how to shape specific policy objectives. Many European states have strong relations with their old colonies and wish to shield them from economic and political pressures, for both selfish and prestige reasons. States cannot entirely ignore questions of commercial advantage, particularly in situations where strategic minerals, such as oil or uranium, are concerned. Among European states, for instance, France and Portugal were notably less enthusiastic than others about political conditionalities in general, and tended not to make a fuss about them in their direct dealings with African states, though they did go along with them in multilateral settings. The upshot of all these complications was a set of conditionalities, both economic and political, that did not seem to work very well, that were only fitfully maintained by some states some of the time, and that were open to accusations of arbitrariness and inconsistency, even contradiction. How, after all, can one *impose* democracy on others?

A second difficulty with conditionalities was that the sheer scale of post-Cold War engagement with Africa, and the increasing proliferation of development agencies, made coordination nigh on impossible. By the 1990s, there was a much larger number of aid donors, including states, international organisations and NGOs, offering a bewildering variety of different types of aid, projects and programmes. Every one of these agencies had their own agendas, constituencies and operating procedures. As a result, there was often massive duplication of activity. In Sierra Leone, for example, by the time the war ended in 2002 there were forty-two donor agencies at work. About 65% of aid was channelled through government agencies: 20% to UN agencies, and 15% through NGOs. Seventeen UN agencies were involved in the country, fourteen of them having offices there. Some ninety-five international NGOs were engaged in various projects. Sometimes this proliferation was so intense as to develop into outright competition with different agencies battling against each other for funds.

This proliferation and competition among agencies made for a third difficulty in that it opened up sometimes considerable space for African states to play off donors against each other. On occasion, major donors disagreed among themselves. Sometimes they disagreed with the international financial institutions and were in a position to get their way. The World Bank and the IMF did not always see eye to eye and were subject to different kinds of political pressures. Both states and international organisations experienced intense scrutiny and criticism from NGOs which themselves commanded increasingly large resources. This left quite a bit of room for African states to appeal to one group of donors then another, to raise some kinds of policy issues with particular donors, to appeal for political support from NGOs against the IFIs, to propose certain types of project to certain donors knowing they would get a sympathetic hearing. Tough conditions were imposed on Mozambique in the 1990s, with the IMF demanding huge cuts in public spending, whereas the World Bank wanted improvements in public sector pay. In 1995, IMF demands for cuts in the minimum wage led to a donor revolt against the IMF, and its harsh policies were gradually eased, with a resumption of growth in the Mozambican economy. So, although the period of structural adjustment did produce a much greater ability of Western agencies to interfere in African countries, it remained patchy, often modified by their donor politics, and sometimes undermined by other donors. Partly for these reasons African governments retained some room for manoeuvre. The least dependent could resist, if only by dragging their feet. But countries in desperate straits could find themselves exposed to increasingly intrusive interference from the BWIs.

A COORDINATED RESPONSE

While all these factors made it harder to achieve consistency in the imposition of conditionalities, fairly determined efforts were made through 'international regimes' or 'global governance'. This is where states agree to a set of rules, norms and guidelines that place limits on their sovereignty and facilitate coordination of policy. There are many reasons why states might agree to such limits. Sometimes they are rooted in an overwhelming consensus on matters of principle or fundamental security, as in the cases of piracy and the slave trade in the nineteenth century, which are the oldest examples of such conventions. But more usually, states calculate that restrictions will have compensatory benefits. International regimes vary enormously in their form and scope. They may take a strong form, with a binding legal force – the International Atomic Energy Agency, for example, has certain powers to monitor nuclear energy activity. More usually they come in weaker versions which specify objectives that states broadly agree to without necessarily committing themselves to particular courses of action. In the African context, they have tended to come about as a result of complex relations between states, international organisations and NGOs. It takes considerable political and diplomatic effort to devise such regimes and make them work, but by the 1990s there were two areas, conflict and development, where regimes were feasible. What these regimes have tried to put into effect is benchmarking and coordination – that is, they have tried to set common standards and to call on major players to adhere to those standards.

One of the first, and certainly the best known, was the Kimberley Process. This regime attempted to regulate the diamond trade, which was financing conflict, notably in Angola and Sierra Leone. The diamond trade was first publicised by NGOs because its symbolic significance in the West provided a perfect opportunity to promote the idea that these conflicts were reducible to a battle between good and evil. Two reports in particular, by Global Witness (1998) and Pan-Africa Canada (2000), attracted considerable publicity beyond political media, and even provided the theme for the Hollywood film *Blood Diamond*. This publicity exposed the traditional secrecy of the diamond industry and helped persuade the UN Security Council to impose sanctions on diamond exports from Angola in June 1998, from Sierra Leone in July 2000, from Liberia in March 2001, and from Côte d'Ivoire in December 2005. It also established expert panels to report on the illicit diamond trade. South Africa is a major diamond producer and, fearing a consumer boycott, the South African government convened a meeting of industry, NGOs and others in Kimberley, in May 2000, to discuss ways of stopping the trade in conflict diamonds. This resulted in a regulatory agreement – the Kimberley Process Certification Scheme (KPCS) – designed to ensure that shipments of rough diamonds crossing an international border are transported in a sealed container and accompanied by an official certificate. Such shipments can only be exported to another Kimberley Process participating country, and the importing country must check the contents of the shipment. If shipments do not meet stringent requirements they may be confiscated. The diamond industry, through the World Diamond Council, must provide evidence to all purchasers of diamonds that they are from conflict-free sources. Countries participating in the scheme must have robust national laws to monitor the production and trade in diamonds, and countries which do not meet the scheme's standards can be suspended from membership.

Although the conflicts in Angola and Sierra Leone were resolved, resources were now a dimension in other conflicts. Although nothing had quite the publicity impact of diamonds, the mineral 'coltan' (strictly columbite-tantalite) had a similar profile, as it is used in the manufacture of mobile phones. One of the main areas of supply is the eastern regions of the Democratic Republic of Congo, which has been a zone of considerable conflict since 1999. Other regional powers, notably Uganda and Rwanda, have frequently manipulated the conflict and sometimes become directly engaged in pursuit of their own agendas. These conflicts have been funded, in part, by illicit mining or the 'taxation' of miners by military groups. To block access to these mineral resources, international organisations have fashioned various regulatory schemes, covering either particular minerals such as tin and gold, or manufactured goods like jewellery, or particular regions. Most of these schemes are, however, semi-voluntary. Latterly, the United States has passed legislation (the Dodd-Frank Act) that requires US companies to ensure that materials they use are conflict-free on pain of serious penalties, and this a requirement they must also impose on their suppliers.* The EU is in the process of preparing similar regulations. Broadly speaking, these schemes focus on the misappropriation of revenue by armed groups by diverting resources and revenues through legitimate channels, usually big respectable businesses or states. But of course, big business and states can also misappropriate resources, so attempts have been made to extend the 'regime' model to other kinds of resource transactions that do not involve conflict.

We can see here yet another example of how the 'economic' and 'political', the 'international' and 'domestic', have become increasingly interconnected. The attempts to set up resources

---

* I should add that, at the time of writing, this legislation is being challenged in the United States on legal and constitutional grounds.

regimes were partly about economic efficiency, but also partly about making information available so that enterprises and states could be held to account. The most elaborate is the Extractive Industries Transparency Initiative (EITI), launched in 2002 in Johannesburg by former British Prime Minister Tony Blair. It is a voluntary coalition of states, international organisations, business organisations and NGOs, which claims to set a global standard for transparency in the oil, gas and mining industries. The EITI encourages companies to disclose what they pay to states, and payments and receipts are independently audited and made public.

While the debates about structural adjustment and resource conflict raged on, Western public opinion had become increasingly distressed about poverty. IMF programmes, concerned as they were with what governments spend, paid little heed to the distributional consequences. But for many African governments the easiest budgets to cut were the public sector wage bill and social welfare. Although it is still not clear whether cuts were hitting the poor, it came to be widely accepted that there was a problem, and the BWIs started to provide some African countries with additional resources to alleviate the impact of structural adjustment on the least well-off. Nor did these criticisms come only from the 'usual suspects': the Bank acquired a new head in 1995, James Wolfenson, whose first official speech drew attention to poverty. The Bank's mission was redefined as fostering a 'world without poverty'. In 1997, the new British Labour government created the Department for International Development (DFID) as a separate department, replacing the Overseas Development Administration (ODA), which had been part of the Foreign Office. Its first permanent secretary said the mission of the Department was the elimination of world poverty. The first White Paper published by the Department had the same title. As always, there were also more prosaic factors in play. By the mid-1990s the World Bank, and to some extent the IMF, had reached something of an impasse. Both had encountered extensive criticism of their handling of the 1997 Asian financial crisis, which had severely damaged their credibility. Another line of criticism focused on the steady accumulation of additional debts by many African countries which, it was widely conceded, were never going to be repaid. The debt issue became the object of an extraordinarily successful campaign led by an advocacy group, Jubilee 2000, which brought heavy pressure to bear on the IFIs to consider measures of debt forgiveness, pressure to which they eventually had to accede.

These various pressures brought about a shift in the direction of the BWIs, leading to a new approach in early 1999 called the Comprehensive Development Framework. There was a much greater and more explicit commitment to the elimination of poverty, in line with the Millennium Development Goals. To that end new resources would be made available for development and especially for debt cancellation for the poorest states. Many donors now acknowledged that aid had become excessively fragmented and unduly complicated. At various international meetings, donors signalled that aid would continue, indeed would increase, but also that much of it would be distributed through national budgets, rather than earmarked to particular projects. These new policies were articulated in an idiom of 'partnership', suggesting that the givers and receivers of aid were engaged in a common enterprise, rather than donors telling countries what to do. The harsh, explicit language of 'conditionality' was to be abandoned and replaced by a language of 'ownership', 'dialogue', 'participation' and 'stakeholders'. This partnership came with a price of, course – and it was this that represented a new kind of 'soft' international regime. The new framework required that developing countries explicitly commit to, and be held accountable for, policies that reduced poverty. This policy would be implemented by means of a new document, called a Poverty Reduction Strategy Paper (PRSP), in which a government would have to outline its goals and explain how it intended to achieve them. This document would need to be accepted by both the IMF and the World Bank. In this way, PRSPs quietly extended conditionality beyond the content of policies to the process of policymaking itself. This approach demanded that the elite 'own' the policies and ensured that 'civil society' kept the elite up to the mark (the rhetoric of 'participation'). So African governments were required to demonstrate what steps they had taken to consult 'civil society' organisations in the preparation of their policies and programmes.

Perhaps the most remarkable example of the ambition of some international organisations was the World Bank's role in the Chad–Cameroon pipeline, an involvement that came close to being a kind of trusteeship. Chad, a country in central Africa, grossly neglected by its French colonial masters, became independent in 1960. Landlocked, about five times the size of the UK but with a population of less than 15 million, it comes near the bottom of virtually every development indicator, and has been plagued by conflict since independence. Oil was known to exist in the 1970s, but exploitation only became possible in the 1990s. The main practical issue was how to get the oil to market, since this would require a 1,000 kilometre pipeline to Cameroon.

Along with all the attendant construction work for pumping stations and other essential infrastructure, the project cost $4 billion, the largest single investment in Africa at the time. The vast bulk of these funds came from oil companies but, given the political sensitivities (a number of NGOs vociferously opposed the project), they had insisted the World Bank participate. So the World Bank played a major role in getting the project off the ground and contributed about 10% of the cost. But it also wished to showcase the pipeline as an example of how resources could transform a desperately poor country into a relatively prosperous one. To that end, it put together an elaborate

set of institutions and controls to ensure that the Chad government would spend the bulk of the oil revenue on poverty-reducing
activities in five designated areas: education, health, rural development, infrastructure and water. Another portion was to be
set aside in a future fund, and another to compensate the area
where the oil was being extracted. What little was left would go
into the government's own account. The Bank insisted all this
was written into Chadian law in 1998 before any oil had started
to flow. How could this be done? First, the oil revenue went into
a special account in London which the Bank controlled. Second,
two committees were set up, one external and one internal, both
independent of the Chad government, to ensure that it was held
to its commitments. The internal committee had to include
representatives of 'civil society'. This elaborate scheme failed to
work, and quickly became mired in allegations of bribery and
profits being used by the government to fund arms sales. The
Chad–Cameroon pipeline represented the most serious attempt
by Western organisations to tighten conditionalities on African
elites in the cause of development, and it failed.

LOCAL ALLIES?

In contrast to the Chad case, the conflict resources regimes
were aimed largely at weaker insurgent groups who were in all
sorts of ways weaker than states, and in some respects they
succeeded. The contrast was instructive. Consensus positions
against insurgent groups, particularly if the insurgents use
abhorrent methods, can usually be made to hold. Imposing
constraints on states, even weak ones, is much more difficult.
Western opinion has vacillated on this issue, sometimes tending
to the more punitive view that African elites can be more or
less coerced into following the 'right' policies, and sometimes
tending to the view that elites or sections of elites have to be

co-opted somehow into 'pro-reform' positions. This dilemma is entirely understandable. Although, on occasion, Western agencies could be ruthless in their demands, and damaging in their actions, the fact was that they were not prepared to push African states to the brink by breaking off aid completely. Though threats to aid did occasionally work, as in Kenya in 1992, there were real limits to them. President Moi went on to win two elections under a multiparty system that he openly despised. Much of the threat to withdraw aid had a theatrical element. Only certain kinds of aid would be withdrawn, or only for a limited time, and African elites knew this. There was a residual respect for sovereignty, even among African states, however much that had been eroded in fact. In some circumstances economic and political calculation played a part, particularly if the collapse of a government might cause wider domestic or regional disorder. In some cases more self-interested motives were at work, especially where these concerned crucial commodities or markets. This seems to have been the case with Chad, where US and French lobbying protected the government from pressures to reform. Lastly, the hugely enhanced influence of international NGOs, dramatically demonstrated by the success of Jubilee 2000,* could not be ignored and, while such organisations were not averse to denouncing Africa's political leaders, they generally spoke out against excessive pressure on African states. Indeed, the renewed concern with poverty, and the 'softer' language of partnership and dialogue, did not sit comfortably with strategies of coercion.

For all these reasons then, co-opting African elites remained an attractive strategy; the cultivation of local allies had been part of Western engagement with Africa from independence, and even in colonial times. There is a long history of trying to shape bureaucratic elites (what the World Bank calls 'capacity-

---

* Jubilee 2000 was a coalition of NGOs across dozens of countries, which successfully lobbied for debt cancellation on a large scale.

building'). One of the major problems the BWIs had long faced was that many African states lacked senior officials who were not only competent but also broadly sympathetic to the goals of the BWIs. Considerable efforts were made to train such officials in their image. These efforts ranged from formal training in the prestigious economic departments of Western universities, to the appointment of promising African candidates to senior positions in the World Bank and the IMF (from which they often returned to appointments in their own countries), as well as pressuring African states to appoint such individuals to lead the civil service. African government departments that played ball often got additional aid to acquire modern technology, better working conditions and higher rewards.

The real objective was to win hearts and minds. A good example of these processes at work is Tanzania, whose relations with the World Bank in particular had reached a low ebb in the 1980s, and only began to improve when the new president, Ali Hassan Mwinyi, replaced Julius Nyerere (who had resisted Western policies), and began to appoint sympathetic people to significant positions in the Ministry of Finance. In 1995, the new World Bank director for East Africa was instrumental in influencing the appointment of 'pro-reform' officials to the Office of the President and the Ministry of Finance. The same people set up or worked for influential private consultancies, tended to identify with Western institutions and policies, and had little interest in the political aspects of economic questions, seeing them as purely technical issues. This new breed of technocrat set up their own NGOs, which not only attracted Western support but also gradually developed into a network of people across government, the private sector and academia, who all tacitly supported the BWIs.

With the transition to multiparty democracy, donors began to concentrate resources on political parties, 'think tanks' and civil society groups that focused on economic policy. Donors began to talk of 'social action coalitions', 'reform coalitions', 'growth coalitions', or 'drivers of change' or 'change agents'. Other institutions that attracted interest from donors included the court system and anti-corruption bodies. Often donors substantially designed, organised and financed these institutions, encouraging the membership of state officials and local NGOs. The Nigerian Economic and Financial Crimes Commission (EFCC), set up in 2002 under dynamic chairman Nuhu Ribadu, attracted considerable outside support from the EU, European governments, the World Bank, and the United Nations Development Programme (UNDP). The bulk of these funds went on the establishment of a Training and Research Institute and data centre at the EFCC's headquarters, while the US provided training for 800 prosecutors. At times, external funding allowed the EFCC to continue investigations it could not have otherwise pursued.

As the restoration of multiparty democracy revived the importance of parliamentary institutions, these institutions also began to attract attention. The methods used to build up local allies were essentially financial, either by way of financial support or training. Despite a considerable rhetorical stress on the virtues of participation and accountability, there was little interest in actual local politics and concerns, and certainly not with any politics that might contradict Western institutions. Rather, the idea was to encourage groups that shared a belief in the Western consensus and would help to bring about the goals of the West.

6

CHANGING CONDUCT

WITHIN A DECADE OF THE END of the Cold War, the West had fashioned a veritable arsenal of initiatives designed to bring about change in African societies, modelled on the norms and practices of Western societies. Setting aside the colonial period and the rather special circumstances of the postwar occupation of Germany and Japan, they constituted an historically unprecedented effort by one group of countries to change another group of countries, in some sense for their own good. Yet they seemed to have produced depressingly meagre results.

They were not always thought-through, nor consistent; indeed, they were on occasion vitiated by bad faith and crude understandings of commercial or strategic advantage. Macroeconomic reforms restored some stability to African economies, and there were some improvements in economic indicators more generally. Welfare standards recovered slightly from the declines of the 1980s. Some of the worst tyrants had departed, and there had been some recovery of political freedoms. Yet progress had not exactly been rapid. African economies remained fragile, the continent seemed to be remarkably conflict prone, birth rates remained stubbornly high, huge volumes of resources were smuggled out of the continent, and many qualified Africans departed in search of a better life.

There were two parallel responses to this state of affairs. Both drew on the intuition that financial aid, military intervention, economic and political conditionalities, international regimes, even pliant local allies remained ultimately external to African states, and therefore insufficient to bring about real change. Both reactions were extremely ambitious. Both pointed to a need for even more extensive involvement in the fabric of African societies than had ever been contemplated.

The first response, the more modest and the more optimistic of the two, continued to work through the idea that elites were the source of the problems. Its novelty lay in how these problems were to be resolved, which was to encourage African societies to make African elites more accountable, obliging them to attend to the business of 'development'. So this strategy looked to politics and political institutions, following a path already opened up by conditionalities, but involving an even deeper intrusion into African political systems, indeed towards the fundamental reorganisation of African states. It would no longer be enough to advise or put pressure on the various parts of the African state; it would be necessary to completely reconfigure the relations between its constituent parts. This involved more than telling African states what they should do; it meant telling them *how* they should do it. Rhetorical commitments to democracy, even real elections, would no longer suffice. Rather, democratisation had to be understood as a complete reorganisation of the relations between state and society.

But there was a second response, more pessimistic and even more radical in its implications than the first. This stemmed from an almost unmentionable intuition that Africa's problems might be rooted as much in African societies as in African elites. The questions it posed, if not the answers, were unavoidable. If social forces hold states and elites to account, were there any guarantees that the social forces in play would actually perform that role? This response required going beyond the purely political. It meant engaging directly with society. A modern state can only work in a context of modern social groups, and such groups must be inclusive, egalitarian, democratic and participative, all in the spirit of (contemporary) Western modernity. But that would point to the most difficult challenge of all, what one World Bank expert memorably called the long-term process of 'changing mentalities'.

These intuitions, and their strategic implications, are very abstract and extraordinarily ambitious. They are shared to very different degrees by a wide range of agencies, some taking them seriously, others less so. In certain quarters, even if they are not publicly repudiated, they are viewed as excessively ambitious. Even among their proponents there is vigorous disagreement about priorities, resources and methods. But something like a common core remains: between them, these agencies are putting into place, in Africa, a liberal, Western social order.

SWEDEN OR DENMARK ON A GOOD DAY, PERHAPS?

With the revival of the ideas of the 'standard of civilisation', sovereignty could be understood as a matter of degree, rather than an absolute condition. The ways in which sovereignty had been eroded were usually justified by special circumstances, such as attacks on civilian populations or 'special case' issues like conflict minerals. None of these situations had warranted a routine, continual, deep engagement with the political structures and processes of African societies, an engagement that would make it virtually impossible to avoid acknowledging a substantial breach in the sovereignty of African states. There was, however, an ingenious alternative to that unwelcome possibility – the notion of 'governance'.

The jokey definition of governance offered by Harvard academic Dr Matt Andrews, 'Sweden or Denmark on a good day, perhaps', tells us rather more than the kind of 'serious' definitions encountered in policy papers and conferences (such as 'forms of collective regulation of social circumstances' or 'patterns of regulating interdependence'). What 'governance' enabled people to do was to get round the problem of sovereignty and politics. The British government does not tell the French government how to run its affairs, much less how to manage its state. But African states were to be instructed, while preserving, at least, the niceties of sovereignty. So 'governance', almost like magic, broke the taboo of opening up the African state to a much more intrusive Western surveillance. This required a more detailed knowledge of the structure of state institutions, not just in the sense of how they were supposed to work, the rules and procedures laid down on paper, but how they *really* worked, who *really* made policy and decisions, and who *really* controlled resources.

To understand these things in any state structure it is necessary to know how different institutions and organisations fit together, how they collaborate with or (equally often) obstruct each other, which parts of the bureaucracy really are powerful, and which are decorative. It is even necessary to know about, and intervene in, the dynamics between state institutions and wider society. This kind of detailed knowledge of a whole society is something we only ever hold over our own countries. More than knowledge, it is something like experience. Much of that knowledge and experience is informal because, whatever the social differences between members of any society, they will still have a great deal in common. States have slowly learnt what is and isn't possible; what can and cannot be done. Successful modern states work in large part because they have successfully reshaped the wider society. The situation is dramatically different in circumstances where attempts are being made to bring about changes in a wholly different society without such local experience. The main consequence is that there can be no limits either to what needs to be known about the target society, or the scope of intervention within it. Knowledge of, and intervention in, one area only triggers the need for intervention in other areas.

Like most things in the world of development, the concern with 'governance' did not represent a complete break with the past. The World Bank had been funding civil service projects for many years. It set up a 'public sector management team' as early as 1983. From time to time it referred to 'governance' in reports, but very little systematic attention was devoted to these issues before about 2000. By then, however, the Bank, along with other agencies, had decided it needed to know much more about how African states really worked, so from the 1990s this engagement was on a much larger scale, attracted much more funding, and developed several important innovations. The point of such exercises was not simply to acquire knowledge but to actually exert influence and bring about change. So once 'governance' had become a legitimate label it wasn't long before various agencies began to develop a whole series of governance 'indicators' and 'benchmarks', and to use such measures to shape policy. But these governance indicators rapidly outstripped the notion of governance as limited to (even in the broadest sense) the institutions of government, and started to encompass almost every aspect of social and political life. The British DFID pioneered a programme called 'Drivers of Change', whose objective was to understand political systems and the mechanics of 'pro-poor change', and, in particular, the role of formal and informal institutions in enabling or hampering such change. The EU's 'governance profile' of a state includes such matters as 'government effectiveness' and 'economic governance', but also elections, human rights, the rule of law, political stability, regional integration and much else besides. The World Bank's World Governance Indicators, one of the standard 'measures', includes thirty different elements. The implausibility of all this notwithstanding, governance began to

appear everywhere: academics cooked up degrees in it and jour-
nals in which to write about it; virtually all international
development organisations trumpeted it as part of their new
commitments. The European Union actually wrote it into the
text of the Cotonou Treaty, which covers trade and political
relations between the European Union and seventy-nine African,
Caribbean and Pacific states.

Where academics and institutions pointed, resources soon
followed. Official Development Assistance (ODA) from OECD
countries allocated to government and civil society reached
around $5 billion, amounting to 9% of ODA, compared to 0.5%
in 1980. By the year 2000, the World Bank was spending
$2 billion a year on governance projects, and four years later
nearly $4 billion. Between 1995 and 2004, the Bank lent around
$9 billion and gave another $1 billion in grants for public sector
capacity-building. With programmatic statements and resources
in place, the way was then open to inscribe governance issues
into project and general lending. The European Union has led
the way in this area through a device called the Governance
Incentive Tranche, a fund layered to provide additional rewards
to states that submit an acceptable Governance Action Plan. In
2007, the World Bank announced a Governance and Anti-
Corruption Strategy as part of a drive to 'mainstream' governance
across its operations. Much World Bank aid is now processed by
means of a Partnership Strategy, and special funds have been
created to enable country strategies to consider governance issues.

Of all the projects that the governance agenda has inspired,
the largest in scale, resources and effort has been the 'decentralisation' of government. While the definitional disputes about
this idea are lively, the basic point is clear enough, and concerns
the way in which power and resources are shared between central
and local authorities. But why the popularity of the idea for
Africa? Decentralisation seemed to be the holy grail that could
transform everything for the better. A number of arguments

were regularly rehearsed. The first was that the lack of interest in development on the part of African states would change once there were active local authorities which were 'closer to the people' and therefore better able to understand and articulate their needs and aspirations. They would also be better placed to respond to, and be held accountable by, the ultimate beneficiaries. The second argument concerned the marginalisation and exclusion of certain groups, problems which could be overcome once power was devolved to the level of 'the people' and thus made more inclusive. All voices would be heard. A third argument suggested that conflict resolution and better service provision would greatly enhance popular participation, which would in turn contribute to the consolidation of democracy. All of these claims chimed with a growing fashion, after the era of structural adjustment, for 'bottom-up' or 'participatory' development, the idea being that things only work if they attract the support of local communities.

Such a dazzling set of possibilities proved irresistible. Donor agencies produced a steady stream of policy documents, reports and recommendations, calling for schemes of decentralisation. By 2002, the UNDP was actively supporting decentralisation in some ninety-five countries, many of them in Africa. No one seems to know exactly how much has been spent on decentralisation projects, but no one doubts that it is a lot. Between 1990 and 2007, the World Bank spent over $7 billion on decentralisation programmes in twenty developing countries. In Liberia, the UNDP administers funds for a Decentralisation Support Programme. In Burundi, the World Bank, the European Union and Swiss aid agencies deliver decentralisation programmes, with much of the funding for the new local authorities provided by donors and NGOs. When Malawi embarked on a decentralisation programme, seventeen donors were involved. By 2002, about thirty countries in Africa were implementing decentralisation schemes. Uganda has been one of the major destinations for such funding. The UN and the World Bank first chipped in some $80 million, which was followed by a much larger programme of $165 million. Between 1987 and 2007, the US provided some $2.5 billion in economic assistance to Uganda, a substantial proportion of which was for decentralisation projects.*

But, as the Uganda case showed, and as so often in the 'development' project, distributing money was only the beginning. Virtually all decentralisation schemes compelled the donors to burrow ever deeper into the structures of African politics. New structures means new complications. Central government departments had to be forced to give up powers. In Sierra Leone, the World Bank demanded that the health ministry be decentralised before allocating health funds. And the new local councils in Sierra Leone did not align with traditional chiefdoms, so special arrangements had to be made. In Uganda, health districts did not coincide with existing administrative divisions. Everywhere, decentralisation schemes required that relations between old and new structures of government had to be monitored and guided.

It is easy enough to sign big cheques in Washington, London or Brussels, but decisions have to be made about where exactly the money is to go, and who is to account for it. Quite frequently the devising of new institutions allows for the possibility of 'elite capture', where local officials exploit new positions and resources for salaries, buildings and other perks of office. (Calls are then inevitably made for anti-corruption commissions.) On top of this, new structures need new training, facilities and equipment. This is not just a question of learning how to work a computer or an accounting system, but new kinds of attitudes and dispositions, often labelled under the nebulous term 'behavioural change'. New decentralised structures must also have something to distribute. So in Uganda, probably the African country most committed to decentralisation (indeed before it became a donor

---

* Known as Strengthening Decentralisation in Uganda (SDU) I and II.

fashion), the World Bank funded an Institutional and Infrastructural Development Project in Kampala. The project, which began in 2007, provided $34 million to Kampala City Council to restructure its administration and management, improve service delivery, image and public relations. Other donors, for example Belgium, provided funds for environmental management, as did NGOs such as WaterAid's 2011–16 strategy to improve water and sanitation for the urban poor.

Lastly, decentralisation is supposed to be about the people and their choices. But those choices have to be funded. So the donors found themselves providing funds for people to make choices. Variously called 'social action' funds, 'social capital' funds or development funds, these needed to be publicised. So donors found themselves funding the publicity efforts. Part of the job of the (donor-funded) National Initiative for Civic Education in Malawi was to tell people how to apply for donor funds. All of these issues – institutions, money, capabilities and know-how, politicians – were completely interlocked. The real consequence of opening up 'governance' was that there was nowhere to stop.

DEMOCRACY

Much the same dynamic applied to democratisation. Governance and democratisation were intended to be complementary. Twenty-five years ago, political change in Africa was thought to be relatively straightforward. The disappearance of the one-party state and the reintroduction of multiparty politics and competitive elections would bring about new governments which were committed to development and would be held accountable in future elections. As we noted earlier, Western powers began to call for the reintroduction of multiparty elections almost as soon as the Cold War ended. The predominance of the West after the end of the Cold War, and the collapse of the idea of the one-party state, ensured that change followed very rapidly indeed. In 1991, hardly any African states had regular multiparty elections (Botswana has always been the big exception), and not a single African government had changed hands as the result of an election. Within a few years, most African states had held multiparty elections, and a few had even had changes of government as a result. So elections held great appeal for donors. They are dramatic, visible events; they are relatively easy to organise; they seem to produce political consensus; and they can be played as a success to metropolitan audiences and used to justify aid.

The first phase of democratisation focused energies on the administration and funding of elections. Elections are expensive. They need, and they get, big money. In Uganda, donors financed 70% of the 1993 constituent assembly elections, covered the bulk of the cost of the 1996 presidential and parliamentary elections, and about half the cost of the 2001 district elections and the 2003 elections. In the Congo, the EU spent about €750 million on the 2006 elections. Donors funded about a third of the cost of Malawi's 2004 elections, and some 40% of both the 2009 and 2014 elections. But while it was true that ruling parties, many of which had atrophied in the absence of political competition, now had to renew their mandates by winning elections, it did not take long for many African elites to see that while they might have to adapt to the new reality, there were various ways they could hang on to power.

So, in practice, few African ruling parties changed as a result of the elections. Many remained what political scientists call dominant party systems, allowing (more or less) open political competition and (more or less) genuine elections, but using their command of the state to make it difficult, if not impossible, for opposition parties to win. Further, there was little sign that multiparty elections had produced huge gains in political participation, never mind accountability. First elections often achieved very high turnouts, but turnout later declined. Newly elected parliaments had little power over governments; political parties engaged in little policy debate and only really mobilised people at election times.

Over time, then, it became clear that elections were not enough. Elections work in established democracies because they have developed over time and are embedded in a whole series of supporting institutions and practices. Most of these were absent in Africa. So, just as with governance, the goal of establishing 'democracy' required Western donors to move beyond the core activities of elections, first to the electoral cycle, and then to the wider democratisation of society as a whole. And, just as with governance, there are virtually no limits to how far this engagement may go. Even the maintenance of the electoral cycle requires long-term commitment to complex bureaucratic processes of constituency delimitation, candidate nomination, voter registration, and the drafting of electoral regulations. As the DFID put it: 'If we are serious about supporting democratic development, we need a long-term engagement throughout the development of the electoral system, grounded in careful analysis of the power dynamics and political constraints.'* But there also needs to be more effective political organisation. Political parties need a fee-paying membership to fund their activities, but better elections also need policy debate and the dissemination of policy. That, in turn, means not just a free press, but financially viable policy institutes and publications, and all these will be a waste of time if they have no impact on parliament and government. But for parliament to hold government to account, there must be informed MPs who have some control over parliamentary procedure. There also need to be parliamentary research facilities and time made available to allow debate.

Donor funding gradually swung into line with this inexorable logic. The United Nations set up a democracy fund in 2005. The

---

* DFID report 'How to Note: On Electoral Assistance', December 2010, p. 1.

United States used two agencies, the congressionally funded National Democratic Institute, and an Office of Democracy and Governance as a special section within the main aid agency – the United States Agency for International Development (USAID). By 2005, USAID had missions in twenty-three African countries. The European Union developed the European Initiative (now Instrument) on Democracy and Human Rights which, by 2006/7, was spending about €2.5 billion. These resources could be used to fund non-state actors without a state's consent. Aside from these EU initiatives, the Netherlands has an Institute for Multiparty Democracy, and the UK has the Westminster Foundation. Germany has *Stiftungen* (foundations), linked to political parties and publicly funded, which they may spend on projects and organisations which are congruent with their ideological leanings. They are now running programmes in some thirty African countries. Other Western organisations, such as lawyers' groups and journalists, have also seen it as part of their role to promote democracy in African states. By 2005, according to some estimates, spending on democracy promotion was running at £5 billion a year.

These funds were focused on three broad areas: political parties and parliaments; the media; and electors. The attention given to parties and parliaments, both explicitly partisan polit-ical bodies, showed that any residual coyness about getting involved in 'politics' had been abandoned. Resources were now directed towards parties themselves to make them more effective as organisations (but also more internally democratic), to enable them to deal with other organisations, and to equip them to function more effectively within the local political system. It was important not merely to make political parties more effec-tive as organisations, but also to make them more effective within the framework of parliamentary government, to ask questions in parliament, criticise government policy, scrutinise public spending and budgets, and to hold governments 'to account'. Similarly, their electoral capabilities needed to be enhanced so they could engage with the public, articulate political programmes, produce propaganda and attract membership. In pursuit of these goals, political parties in Africa were provided with financial and technical assistance in the form of seminars, workshops and meetings, the training of leaders, research and polling activities, visits and tours to parliaments and political parties in the West.

The sheer scale of this engagement defies easy summary. In Ghana, USAID, the United Nations Development Programme (UNDP), the Canadian International Development Agency (CIDA), the European Union (EU), and the Netherlands Institute for Multiparty Democracy (NIMD) all financed the electoral system, from ballot papers and identification cards to transparent ballot boxes, election observation projects and parallel vote counts. USAID and German foundations organised parliamentary visits and provided support and training for MPs, especially in committees concerned with public finance. German Embassy funding enabled the Ghanaian NGOs to systematically monitor election violence and undertake conflict prevention in northern Ghana and other conflict-prone areas. The UNDP and DFID funded the peace campaigns and conflict-mediation activities of prominent Ghanaian traditional and religious leaders. The EU sponsored extensive voter education programmes undertaken by state bodies such as the National Commission for Civic Education. As one Ghanaian expert, E. Gyimah-Boadi, put it: 'external donors have almost nearly exclusively bankrolled the numerous projects that Ghana's domestic civil society and media have initiated to promote election transparency and credibility since the mid-1990s'.

Likewise in Kenya, donors funded much of the return to democracy in 1992, and subsequently. In Kenya, outside engagement was, if anything, even more extensive. USAID and DFID funded a Parliamentary Strengthening Program. The UNDP played a major role as manager of 'basket funds' – that is, specific pools of money to which a variety of donors may contribute. This included substantial support for the Kenyan Election

Commission. The EU provided substantial support for the multi-donor Governance, Justice, Law and Order (GJLOS) programme: one of the most ambitious governance reform programmes ever tried in Africa, it was supported by a substantial donor basket fund of some €44 million, contributed by fifteen development agencies. This programme comprised activities across a wide range of areas, including law, improved service delivery, anti-corruption activities, improved access to justice for the poor, and a more informed and participative citizenry and non-state actors. There have been a number of international initiatives aiming to strengthen Kenyan political parties. USAID and the (US) National Endowment for Democracy (NED) provided funds to enhance the organisational, parliamentary and election campaign capacities of the main political parties. Special provisions were made for technical assistance for the development of new legislative agendas; training for young, female and Muslim MPs on parliamentary procedure; communications, lobbying and leadership; the training of party secretariats and the development of party policies, manifestos and constitutions; as well as the development of organisational structures and communication between HQ and the various branches. The Dutch government funded the Centre for Multiparty Democracy–Kenya (CMD-K), which was established in 2004 by sixteen major Kenyan political parties to help institutionalise political parties and improve relations between political and civil society.

While these programmes tended to have similar targets, they were by no means the same, and the donors were not insensitive to local political circumstances. Far more aid went to political parties in Ghana than in Kenya where, by contrast, aid was disproportionately directed towards what was being called 'civil society'. Virtually all the big donors in Kenya were involved in supporting civil society. Part of this effort involved grants to Kenyan NGOs. USAID was a major supporter of some of the most prominent ones, including the Kenyan chapters of

Transparency International and the International Commission of Jurists, as well as funding a Kenyan Civil Society Strengthening Programme. DFID ran the Political Empowerment Programme (PEP), funding elections, civic education, and gender-related projects, and also gave grants to Kenyan NGOs. But by far the largest programme in this area was the National Civic Education Programme (NCEP), one of the largest such programmes anywhere in the world, consisting of some 50,000 workshops, lectures, plays, puppet shows and community meetings coordinated by over eighty Kenyan NGOs in order to promote democratic values, awareness and political engagement among ordinary Kenyan citizens in the run-up to the 2002 elections. It is estimated that 4.5 million people attended at least one of the programme's activities. A second phase, taking the name 'Uraia' ('citizenship' in Kiswahili), which ran during 2006–7, financed through a 'basket' fund provided by ten donors, involved approximately 79,000 workshops, as well as informal meetings, cultural gatherings and media stories. One estimate is that this programme reached about a quarter of Kenya's population.

CIVIL SOCIETY

We have already had occasion to encounter in earlier chapters the term 'civil society'. But what exactly is 'civil society', and why did it attract so much attention? Clarity on these questions is not helped by the tendency of donors and many of their academic spokesmen to lump together, as the examples of Ghana and Kenya show, governance, democracy, civil society and human rights. In one sense they are right: there are connections between these things; but we need to be clearer about what they are. Whenever a new word is coined in politics, or an old one revived, we can be sure that something significant is going on. The term 'civil society' was used by social and political thinkers in the eighteenth and nineteenth centuries, but it certainly was not common in the twentieth century, and the sudden explosion in its use from the 1990s had very little to do with reading Hegel or de Tocqueville.

Thinking about Africa in the late twentieth and early twenty-first centuries prompted many observers and analysts to reflect on the precedent of the Soviet bloc countries, especially Eastern Europe. In the face of well-entrenched and repressive regimes, backed by an overwhelmingly powerful and heavily armed ally, resistance movements had emerged which begun to challenge such regimes. Several important features of these movements caught the eye of Western observers. First, they operated outside the political space (from which they were in any case excluded), and partly for this reason they remained distrustful of formal politics. But that meant that while they resented state domination they sought to organise outside it, through a variety of bodies such as student forums, trade unions, literary and cultural associations, newspapers and other media. In some countries, the churches provided cover for these activities. They did not directly attack the state, and certainly not by means of violent confrontation, though they did engage in public demonstrations. There is no need to review here the ways in which the Eastern European communist regimes finally fell, but it seems clear that, by eroding the authority of such regimes, 'civil society' organisations played an important role in bringing them down.

But there was one more feature of this situation that attracted Western observers as it became clear, in Gorbachev's USSR, that some degree of reform in the Soviet bloc was inevitable. From the beginning, Eastern European civil society organisations had accepted Western support of various kinds, which brought with it influence. But they continued to subscribe to a variety of political options. Gradually, however, demands for a change in the Soviet system came to mean its replacement by liberal market capitalism.

So there was an important theoretical dimension – almost by

definition, 'civil society' encapsulates many of the core features of Western liberal thinking about society and politics. The key idea is the notion of pluralism and its implications. Western liberal societies are complex and diverse, comprised as they are of individuals understood to have different interests. A central issue facing such societies is how these interests are to be reconciled. How can people live together more or less at peace and share the benefits of social cooperation? One part of the answer is 'the market', which mediates the interests of individuals through the mechanism of exchange and price. But the market is not suited to the management of all social relations, so another part of the answer is 'civil society', which solves the issue of diverse interests in three main ways. First, it allows for the expression and representation of such interests in social movements and associations. Second, the very existence of organised social activity provides a counterweight to the powers of modern states. Third, civil society is thought to play an educational function in that it encourages organised social interests to respect each other's aspirations and viewpoints, which in turn fosters the peaceful resolution of differences.

So what gave 'civil society' a new lease of life was that it seemed to generalise the experience of the transition to liberal capitalism in Eastern Europe, to make sense of liberal capitalism itself, and to provide a kind of theoretical model of that experience which could be applied elsewhere. Civil society was not just a hypothesis – it had actually worked. Everywhere in Africa, regimes that had had some association with the Soviet bloc, or labelled themselves (however implausibly) as Marxists, either disappeared (Ethiopia, Benin) or quickly changed their colours (Angola, Mozambique, Congo-Brazzaville). Within a couple of years of the fall of the Berlin Wall, it was as though Marxism in Africa had never existed. Against this background the attractions of 'civil society' in Africa made a lot of sense. This combination of historical and theoretical optimism came to see 'civil society' as a sort of cure-all for the ills of previous development efforts. It seemed to connect all the things that were problematic, and promised to resolve them. The World Bank argued that a strong civil society participating in public affairs was an essential component of good governance. USAID emphasised the importance of civil society in creating a democratic culture, and particularly its role as a counterbalance to the exercise of excessive authority by governments and economic and political elites. The British DFID stressed the role of civil society in enabling poor and marginalised groups to participate in decision making, and the role of civil society in providing goods and services to the poor. The Australian government weighed in with arguments that civil society organisations can be powerful agents for change – as partners in the delivery of better services, enabling social inclusion, and making governments more effective, accountable and transparent. And to do that the state's activities must be made as transparent as possible through the provision of information, a free press and public debate, and 'civil society' groups must be 'empowered' so that they can play a key role in pressuring the state for better performance. As the World Bank put it: 'Aware that they are being monitored by citizen groups, public officials know that they may be held accountable for budget discrepancies or failure to deliver adequate services.' President of the World Bank, James Wolfenson, went so far as to suggest that civil society was 'probably the largest single factor in development'.

Donor states and their various think tanks and academic voices rapidly fleshed out 'mission statements', 'strategies' and 'modalities' of the kind that invariably accompany the organisation and legitimisation of such visions and their huge expenditures. The objective of DFID's Civil Society Challenge Fund, which requires a UK-based partner, was to 'improve the capacity of Southern civil society to engage in local and national decision-making processes; improve linkages through global advocacy; or provide innovative service delivery or service delivery in a difficult environment'. The equivalent programme of the Irish government had, as one of its policy objectives, to 'support an enabling environment for civil society to organise and engage with government and its own broader constituencies'. These very general sorts of programmes had to be broken down into specific objectives when they were applied to particular countries. Nor was this simply rhetoric. Donors increased aid provision for 'government and civil society' from just over $2.5 billion in 1989, to nearly $12.5 billion in 2005 (by way of comparison, lending for education was twice as much in 1989, but only two-thirds as much in 2005). Over the same time period, direct support to NGOs nearly doubled, as Western donors increasingly funded cooperation between Western NGOs and civil society groups in developing countries.

Through various forms of pressure, the 'participation' of civil society in the design and implementation of development interventions was expanded, most obviously in the Poverty Reduction Strategy Paper (PRSP) process. With this kind of money sloshing around, it was hardly surprising that established NGOs hustled to get their share, and droves of new ones popped up to get in on the act. This was especially the case within Africa itself. Figures are notoriously unreliable, but one estimate suggests that there were some 8,000–9,000 local NGOs in all of Africa in 1988, while by 2005 nearly 99,000 were registered in South Africa alone. Country figures are more reliable. Kenya, for example, experienced a rapid increase in registered NGOs, from 400 in 1990 to over 6,000 in 2008. Likewise, in Tanzania, the 41 registered NGOs active in 1990 had increased to more than 10,000 by 2000. Estimates varied wildly as to the activities of such organisations. According to Tanzanian newspaper *The Express*, of the 3,500 registered NGOs in the country, only 500 were operational, while the remainder were 'briefcase' NGOs set up merely to funnel funds into their directors' pockets.

It was not long before the sheer scale of the funds involved, as well as these developments, prompted greater scrutiny of the whole civil society strategy – indeed the civil society concept. A number of difficulties soon became apparent. Although the civil society strategy meant that huge sums were allocated to Western NGOs, these often continued to pursue their own agendas which were linked to their home constituencies and support base. These agendas might concern health, water supplies, indigenous people – all manner of things – but they inclined NGOs only to deal with entities that looked like themselves, which indeed they often created. To be fair, this tendency was reinforced by the need for them to meet increasingly stringent accounting requirements imposed by their major donors, Western states and international organisations. The explosion of African NGOs was driven by the availability of resources, rather than any great spontaneous flowering of civil society.

It did not take long before various observers, then donors, were complaining that on virtually every criterion African civil society was not doing what civil society is 'supposed' to do. It was not very representative of the population; it was in no position to, indeed had little desire to, challenge the state; it had little internal democracy; and it remained dependent on Western agencies and their agendas. More critical observers were even more scathing, suggesting that in many ways it was positively dysfunctional in its tendencies to create new forms of inequality, promoting clientelism and corruption among leaders, and even weakening the capacity for collective action.

If Western donors and NGOs have had to concede that their civil society strategies have often done little to reach the mass of ordinary people, then what is the alternative? The main response has been to broaden their range of contact within African societies. A whole new vocabulary has been devised to signal this shift. DFID talks about 'non-traditional civil society'; other agencies use the terminology of 'non-state actors'. These labels themselves tell the story: they are less normative, less demanding and carry less theoretical baggage than 'civil society'.

They are descriptive, aiming to grasp what forms of social action actually exist, rather than what outsiders might deem to be desirable. What tended to drive this development initially was conflict situations, or what are called in aid language 'fragile states'. This acknowledges that, in many such situations, there is not an unambiguous political order in which a central state effectively controls things, but rather a weak central state grappling with all sorts of other actors, tribal and 'traditional' structures, religious groups, militias, secret societies, vigilante groups, commercial organisations, traders or 'big men', all of whom may be exercising some degree of power in society. In conflict situations, there is little alternative but to engage with such actors.

Societies in which outside penetration has been extensive provide the best illustration of these tendencies. The end of the war in Sierra Leone in 2002 brought very extensive involvement by the 'international community' in the country, including formal agreements over policy and institutional changes, and long-term aid commitments with an unusually high concentration of resources on 'governance' issues. These were posed as issues of 'peace-building', terminating conflict, re-establishing order, and creating the conditions that would prevent a return to conflict. But the peace-building agenda committed them to deeper engagement with, and deeper intrusions into, the target society. Donor documents repeatedly expressed the importance of civil society, and it was inscribed into the framework of many programmes, including the decentralisation project, the PRSP, and various public sector reforms. But other donor documents, especially those of the agencies they subcontracted the civil society work to, repeatedly expressed rather different sentiments. The international engagement with Sierra Leone, especially in the context of the overwhelming need to restore basic state functions, produced not one but two sets of discourses and policies about civil society. On the one hand, expressions of the ideal notions of civil society; on the other, a reluctant acceptance of the existence of traditional groups and attendant modes of administration and forms of law enforcement. World Bank studies, for example, openly acknowledged the difficulties in applying notions like civil society to much of Sierra Leone, and differentiated 'traditional' from 'formal' civil society, aware that these categories were not watertight. But the Bank placed considerable emphasis on investigating what modes of rule and dispute resolution people actually use. Report after report insisted that civil society was very weak, entirely dependent on outside support, and characterised by financial mismanagement, and a lack of transparency and gender equity.

What becomes clear is that civil society is not simply 'there', ready to be supported. Much of the policy literature, despite its often emollient tone, makes it clear that these are in many ways pathological societies which need to be fundamentally transformed. It is here that the notion of 'civil society' is stretched to breaking point. It ceases to have any connection with a particular society and becomes rather a template against which any such society is to be measured. It is a constant refrain in the literature on Sierra Leone that women and youth must be 'empowered' or 'emancipated', but it is taken as given that this will be brought about by external agencies. The role of civil society strategies is not to reflect the wider society, but to inform and reshape it in our image.

HUMAN RIGHTS

At their limit, the difficulties of civil society strategies seemed to point to a rather drastic conclusion: that it is necessary to go beyond social groups to target individuals. We arrive at the bedrock of the Western project in Africa, the point at which there is nowhere else to go, the point of 'mentalities'. The issue is no longer the way societies or social groups ought to be, but the way people ought to be. The West would call this 'human rights' and, as with other concepts considered in this chapter, before we can make sense of the impact of this idea on policies towards Africa we need to glance at the theoretical and historical contexts.

It suits human rights promoters to claim that the idea is beyond question, both universally accepted and of overriding importance. 'Rights are trumps', as it is often said. But these claims are deeply implausible; indeed, even the proponents of human rights themselves do not agree between themselves. There are two key questions. First, how do we know we have human rights, and where do they come from? Second, what is the scope of human rights, and how precisely do they apply? To put it politely, the answers to these questions are not very clear, although enquiries about them are often met with incredulity, even hostility. In the theoretical literature there are still attempts to provide quasi-religious arguments for rights or, in a more secular vein, understandings of human nature or arguments based on the imperatives of reason. There are interesting debates, but no consensus. The more common response is to refer the enquirer to various international conventions. But this is not much help because these documents do not all agree either. The Universal Declaration of Human Rights 1948 contains a right to private property, but the two 1966 conventions do not. These ambiguities, in turn, bedevil the problem of scope and priority. Do political rights take priority over social and economic rights? Many respectable schools of opinion, especially in the United States, certainly think so – indeed, also think that the notion of social and economic rights makes little sense, whereas opinion in Europe tends to lean the other way. The African Charter on Human and Peoples' Rights, drafted in 1981, contains much that is familiar. But it also contains parental rights – for example, that children must respect their parents – a right that no Western liberal would find acceptable. The reality is that human rights are not universal truths but compromises hammered out in negotiations between states, and they are constantly changing depending on shifting opinion in the world's more powerful states. In practice, 'human rights' are pretty much what their advocates say they are at any moment in time, which means that their potential scope is limitless.

In addition to these theoretical controversies we must also take note of the way in which rights have become important in domestic and international politics. Although Western states did occasionally use the language of rights in earlier historical periods, it is fair to say that 'human rights' as an international political imperative does not really appear until after the Second World War. Although much of the technical drafting was done during this period, Cold War considerations meant rights were in practice downgraded in importance. It is true that anti-colonial movements in Africa made use of the language of rights, but in a national collectivist way (peoples' rights to freedom from colonial domination), rather than as individual rights (as in the famous American right to 'life, liberty and the pursuit of happiness').

So it was not until the end of the Cold War that rights talk came into its own in international politics, with three rather different effects. One of these we have already touched on – namely, a way of limiting state sovereignty. A second effect was a growing tendency to devise new rights, sometimes by expansive interpretations of existing documents, as in 'children's rights', sometimes by wholly novel categories, as in 'indigenous peoples' rights'. Third, there has been an increasing tendency to use rights language, not just to judge states but whole societies. 'Rights talk' has gone beyond judging relations between state and citizen to encompass relations between citizens. This last point is closely connected with the fact that Western societies, since the Second World War, have seen the appearance of increasingly vociferous rights lobbies around a whole range of issues, whose increasingly well-organised and well-funded lobbying might be aimed at countries and movements overseas.

Having emphasised the novelty of human rights, it might seem odd to turn first to historical continuities for evidence of their impact, but this proves to be illuminating. Recollect the idea of the 'standard of civilisation'. Although much of nineteenth-century opinion saw this idea through the lens of slavery, it was by no means the only practice in Africa that elicited negative commentary and sometimes action. Colonial commentary saw African societies as backward and barbaric. The sharp differences in customs and practices between nine-teenth-century Europe and Africa, as well as the prominence of Christian missionaries in the colonial world, ensured that such matters as family, marriage and sexuality formed a prominent part of such judgements. Of course it was precisely such aggres-sive rhetoric and smug assumptions of superiority that fuelled much of the postcolonial guilt about Africa. But the disdain for, and disapproval of, other people's cultural practices can remain remarkably resilient and end up being reformulated in a different language. This particularly concerns the intimate sphere of human life: gender roles, sexuality, child-rearing, inheritance, family structures and so on. These are all matters in which societies (including Western ones) have varied tremendously, and have often jealously guarded their own particular traditions. In this sphere, aggressively hostile attitudes have revived, indeed intensified, largely as a result of trends in Western societies that have hugely expanded the scope of human rights. Thus a very large number of cultural customs that prevail in various parts of Africa have been condemned as 'Harmful Traditional Practices'. International agencies routinely condemn tradition, culture and religion. The term 'violence' is used in an extremely loose way. What constitutes 'harmful' is defined by expansive interpretations of human rights. The problems of definition and inconsistency that these interpretations involve are routinely elided or ignored. The most extensive of these campaigns has been against what is variously called female circumcision, female genital mutilation, or female genital cutting. Terms like 'atrocity' and 'torture' are routinely used. African parents are supposed to take pleasure in mutilating their own girls. Demands for change have been commensurately aggressive, and 'eradication' and 'banning' are the norm, exactly what British colonial governments tried to do in Kenya in the 1920s and Sudan in the 1950s, without success.

But awareness of historical continuities should not make us lose sight of historical discontinuities. Most African countries inherited from their colonial rulers some form of legal proscription of homosexuality.* These laws reflected the situation in the metropolitan powers in the nineteenth and early twentieth centuries when such practices were widely disapproved of and condemned. Attitudes in the West have changed dramatically since then, and not only have laws proscribing homosexuality been dismantled in many countries, but the argument from rights has justified the legitimacy of homosexual marriage, which several countries have now legalised. In the main, African opinion has not followed this trend, partly because the influence of a more traditional Christianity and Islam remain powerful. In this way, the stage is set for homosexuality to become an international political issue. A number of African states, notably Uganda, Gambia, Malawi and Nigeria, have in recent years introduced or reinforced legislation restricting homosexual activity. African presidents, including those of Gambia, Zimbabwe and Namibia, have bitterly attacked homosexuality and gay organisations. Many others have, if less stridently, refused to accept its legitimacy. Such restrictions and denunciations have been met with extremely hostile responses by Western leaders and organisations, often combined with threats to suspend aid. At the Commonwealth meeting in 2011, the British prime minister, David Cameron, raised the possibility of withdrawing

---

* Francophone Africa was something of an exception to this generalisation.

bilateral aid from African states that did not decriminalise homosexuality. Uganda, another country where public opinion is resolutely hostile to homosexuality, has been harshly criticised by the Canadian government, which has also provided funding for Ugandan gay groups. Attempts were made by the EU in the revision of the Cotonou Treaty to insert a sexual orientation clause, though this was subsequently abandoned in the face of African, Caribbean and Pacific opposition. Some countries that are extremely dependent on aid, for example Malawi, have come under heavy pressure to suspend laws proscribing homosexuality, and to pardon those previously convicted.

These two cases throw a sharp light on the ambition and the methods of the Western project in Africa. In relation to female circumcision, along with many other practices that UN agencies define as harmful, the argument is often made that much opinion in Africa itself is against such practices. There is, of course, some truth in that, but by the same token there is much opinion that is not against such practices. Nonetheless, the arguments can be presented in terms of democracy and modernity and, more prosaically, treaty commitments. Generally, African politicians have gone along with the 'harmful tradition' account, though often regretting their inability to change opinion and practice, or change them quickly, within their own countries. For example, most African countries have now criminalised female circumcision, although the laws are often not rigorously enforced, a fact which suggests that new laws reflect deference to external pressures as much as a domestic consensus. In relation to homosexuality, arguments based on democracy lose all plausibility. Although some countries have decriminalised homosexual practices, the majority have not, and surveys suggest that African public opinion is overwhelmingly hostile to the idea of homosexual rights, even in South Africa whose constitution entrenches such rights. Nor has the South African government, despite that constitution, taken an active position internationally in favour of homosexual rights.

Both these examples suggest that, at its most ambitious and most intrusive, the Western project in Africa is about transforming people in the image of Western modernity. Such a project is often thwarted; practical politics often dictate compromise; the vagaries of international relations, and the fickleness of Western public opinion, shift energies from one campaign to another. Realities intrude: it is simply easier to bomb Libya than Zimbabwe. But underneath these swirling currents and tactical shifts lies a dogged determination to make Africans like us. The damaging consequences of that determination, and the need to abandon it, are the issues to which I now turn.

7

A FAILED PROJECT

So far in this book I have explained how ideas about Africa developed in the recent past, and how those ideas helped to shape the actions the West has taken. It is possible to accept everything I have argued so far and still take the view that, for all its faults, the Western agenda in Africa can be improved and made to work. But few readers will have missed that I (along with many others) am extremely sceptical about whether *any* of the policies pursued towards Africa have done it much good, or indeed have done us any good. The kinds of engagement the West has pursued in Africa more or less since independence – economic aid in its many forms, humanitarian intervention, and the various attempts to change African societies – have failed on their own terms, have produced all sorts of unintended consequences and, as often as not, have made things worse. Beyond these failings, Western policies have had deeper negative consequences amounting to a moral corruption of both the promoters of these policies and their intended beneficiaries. For all these reasons, we need to rid ourselves of a number of complexes and prejudices and take a more clear-headed and realistic view of Africa's place in the world.

THE AID BUSINESS

How much aid has gone to Africa? Allowing for all the disputes about definitions, it is something like $1 trillion over the past sixty-five years. We can be more certain about recent figures. Total Official Development Assistance in 2014 was $136 billion. Sub-Saharan Africa received $36 billion. In the same year Britain, one of the world's largest aid donors and the only large economy to have attained the 0.7% of GDP recommended by the UN, spent £11.4 billion on foreign aid, of which almost 40% went to African countries. Vast resources have been transferred to Africa over a long period of time, far more than to any other part of the world and on a much more generous basis. What have been the results of this historically unprecedented transfer of resources?

There is no reason in principle why countries should not benefit from aid, and there are clearly examples where they have. Aside from that, given the scale of resources transferred to Africa it would be extraordinary if they had not had some effect. The difficulty, of course, is to show cause and effect. In the most general terms, poverty seems to have declined in Africa over the past two decades – the World Bank suggests from 56% in 1990, to 43% in 2012. But the same figures suggest that, because of population growth, there are more poor people in absolute terms, some 330 million in 2012, up from about 280 million in 1990. In recent years, almost all African countries have experienced higher rates of growth; indeed, some have experienced much higher rates. The average has been round about 5% between 2000 and 2010, slowing to about 3% from 2010 to 2015, and now slowing further. Africa's population growth rate is about 2.5%, so the per capita increase is not very impressive. And there is little sign that African countries have begun to transform their productive capabilities beyond the production of raw materials for export. Uganda is generally thought to be a 'good performer'. The country posted a growth rate of 7.3% between 1992 and 2009, and has seen a fairly substantial decline in basic poverty, but there has been no great economic transformation. The vast majority of the population continues to work in agriculture, while the manufacturing share of GDP has actually declined. The country continues to be an exporter of raw materials. Ghana has also posted quite high growth rates of around 5%. In 2007, after a statistical revision of its GDP calculations, it was re-classified as a middle-income country. There has been a substantial reduction in poverty, but it still remains quite high with something like a quarter of Ghanaians living in absolute poverty. Again, there has been no real economic transformation, as Ghana's economy is driven by cocoa, gold and timber and, more recently, oil.

There are furious debates about the causes. Has growth been driven by aid or by other factors? In what ways might aid have helped growth? There are libraries full of sophisticated econometric calculations attempting to answer these questions. The balance of opinion among economists and statisticians is that aid does bring about some growth, but that growth is rather modest. The causal links between aid and growth remain obscure and contested. However, we do know that African countries have benefited from debt relief because less money was drained from their economies and, partly as a result, many African states do appear to have paid more attention to the poor. We can also see that the improved growth rates are largely a result of a booming global economy driven by, among other things, a rapidly industrialising China buying raw materials. So a balanced assessment might be that aid has had some impact on poverty, probably does not explain much growth, and has done little if anything to bring about economic transformation.

How can such huge volumes of resources, supplied from largely benign motives, not have a greater effect? Much aid has been wasted. Africa is littered with the remains of ill-thought-out development projects, particularly in the decades immediately after independence. In Tanzania, a shoe factory intended to produce shoes for export to Italy, which within a year of opening was operating at 4% capacity and exporting nothing; a pulp and paper factory which operated at a fraction of its capacity, and whose products cost four times as much as imports; cashew-processing plants with a capacity three times the country's annual crop. In Sudan, a milk dehydration plant was built in an area with no cows, and a sugar refinery that needed 32,000 spare parts from abroad to keep running. In Kenya there was a project to persuade the Turkana, a cattle-herding people, to take up fishing, including the construction of a fish-freezing plant which needed more power than was available in the whole district. In Senegal, a forest barrier of eucalyptus trees was planted to stop the encroaching desert; five years later it had turned to scrub. In Nigeria the Ajaokuta steelworks dates from the 1970s, but has not yet produced any steel. It is easy to poke fun at these absurdities, which were often a result of assumptions of superior judgement, ignorance of local circumstances, bad planning (the Senegalese project had used out-of-date rainfall statistics), and bad implementation. It is fair to say that techniques of analysis have improved, and these kinds of egregious errors are less likely to be made now. But even with more experience and more sophisticated techniques, identifying the benefits of aid projects remains difficult. Just about the only aid projects that work in any straightforward way are those involving health. Campaigns against malaria and river blindness in Africa have worked because there is real scientific understanding of those diseases. Beyond this very narrowly circumscribed set of phenomena, causal connections are complex, and even in well-understood processes there can be disagreements. Deworming of children in Kenya 'works', but the widely cited evidence that deworming school children in Kenya improved school attendance proved, on closer analysis, to be questionable.

A second factor is that much aid is duplicated. Donor priorities can change quite quickly, many donors have complex rules, and procedures for aid disbursement and the demands they make can often conflict with each other. As a result, aid is notoriously difficult to coordinate, and donors often end up doing similar, but separate, projects. This has been a complaint almost from the beginning. As early as 1969 the Pearson Commission on International Development, set up by the World Bank to investigate the effectiveness of its programmes, was critical: 'the present multiplicity of agencies and their lack of coordination lead to much unnecessary duplication of effort.' It called on aid donors to do something about it. Almost forty years later, in 2005, the UNDP echoed plaintively that, 'weakly coordinated donors, many of them operating overlapping programs', were causing serious difficulties. A series of international meetings and conferences were supposed to have overcome these difficulties, but there is little evidence that they have been successful. Part of the reason for this duplication is that NGOs tend to cluster in places where major donors are active, and take less interest in places where there is less donor interest. The Central African Republic gets little aid from donors and receives little attention from NGOs, whereas Malawi gets huge amounts of aid and attention from both. So-called 'donor darlings' can be almost overrun by aid agencies. At any moment in time, Mozambique may be receiving the attention of some 300 NGOs, twelve multilateral organisations, including the UN, twenty or so European donors who are grouped in a Program Aid Partnership, as well as the USA, Japan and a number of 'new' bilateral donors, notably China, India and Brazil. The sheer difficulty of dealing with them all is compounded by the politics of aid. The flow of resources from Western governments (and ultimately their taxpayers) through development agencies and NGOs to the eventual beneficiaries is rarely subjected to much critical scrutiny, and all the parties to these transactions have incentives to report positively. At the level of individual donors and agencies these incentives are even stronger. Evaluation of aid projects is often cursory, since both the dispensers of aid and the evaluators have very good reasons not to be excessively critical.

But what happens to aid when it gets to the beneficiaries? Many aid-funded projects need regular maintenance, which is often neglected or absent. In many parts of Africa a culture of maintenance is not well developed. There is a great deal of coyness about this in discussions of development, and it is usually buried under a label like 'capacity-building', or 'weak management', or 'scarce human resources'. African commentary is often more robust. Olusegun Obasanjo, president of Nigeria from 1999 to 2007, says that 'Africa is poorly managed.'* A glance at almost any sector shows a combination of physical and human factors which make routine maintenance difficult. Report after report on the Nigerian power industry, on which so much aid was spent, details technical inadequacies: some 30% of the power is lost in transmission; transmission and distribution networks are poorly maintained and inefficiently operated; it is possible to connect to the grid without a meter; and the power lines are regularly vandalised. In the circumstances, it is not surprising that Nigerian consumers often do not pay their bills. In a recent speech, the president of Mozambique noted that that in Macomia, Cabo Delgado, a contractor was allowed to simply paint a road black instead of repaving it. Even in South Africa, probably the most technologically sophisticated country in Africa, mainte-

---

* Reported in allafrica.com (2 August 2017): 'Poverty and wealth is a choice Africe must make – Obasanjo' [Online]. Retrieved from http://allafrica.com/view/group/main/main/id/00054253.html (accessed 4 October 2017).

nance practices for water treatment plants and roads are extremely weak.

As we noted earlier, much aid never gets where it is supposed to. In Uganda, a study in 1998 found that less than 30% of resources intended for primary education were actually reaching schools. Similarly, a 2009 study on health spending in Chad showed that less than 1% of non-wage spending ever arrived at primary clinics. Second, even when resources do reach schools or clinics, there are often no teachers or doctors there to use them. A recent report by the African Economic Research Consortium found that health workers in Senegal and Tanzania were absent about 20% of the time. Finally, even when providers are present, the quality of their services is often poor. According to a 2009 World Bank review of public expenditures, teachers in Uganda spend less than 20% of class time teaching. Teachers in Tanzania spend slightly more time on instruction, but only 11% of them have what education experts consider to be the minimum level of language skills required for the job. The situation in the health sector is worse: in Tanzania, the average total amount of time doctors spend seeing patients is only twenty-nine minutes per day.

But even if much aid repeats itself, or leaks away, is it possible that aid can make things worse? In an earlier chapter we discussed how aid not only allowed many African elites to buttress their rule but also enabled them to evade the normal processes by which states secure legitimacy. Those tendencies have by no means disappeared. Aid can weaken the capacities of states because large amounts of aid from a wide array of donor agencies, with different priorities and procedures, make it difficult to maintain budgetary discipline. The actual 'disbursements' of large volumes of aid (when it is handed over, as opposed to when it is promised) are often unpredictable, making planning difficult. Aid is also bound to undermine financial probity. Direct financial aid is the most likely to be diverted, but even project aid enables governments and individuals to pilfer. Corruption associated with public finances is widespread in Africa, endlessly reported on, and shows few signs of going away. And aid induces dependency, where it becomes a kind of substitute for domestic policymaking. Aid brings with it large numbers of advisers and consultants (who do not come cheap), all of which contributes to the poor accountability of African states to their own people, and makes for a lack of credibility in their domestic policies.

'IF YOU KEEP FIGHTING, THE WEST WILL KEEP FEEDING YOU'*

Even if we concede that a huge proportion of these resources is wasted, other forms of engagement with African societies, like humanitarian intervention and attempts to secure 'progressive' social change, must surely be a good thing? Probably the most compelling is humanitarian intervention to prevent conflict and to alleviate its consequences. What could be more important – or more simple – than saving a life? To oppose intervention, even to question it, is to be callous, unfeeling, almost inhuman. But it is the most compelling claims that often need the most scrutiny. There is no reason to impugn the motives of those who call for humanitarian intervention, but there is also no reason to doubt that they are trying to mobilise public opinion and resources, a kind of politics which often resorts to emotional pressure, obscures understanding, and closes down discussion.

And sometimes humanitarian concern does provide cover for other motives. As with development aid, we cannot say that humanitarian intervention can *never* work or *never* does any good – look at the interventions in Mozambique and Sierra

---

* A quote from an aid official in Sudan from Meredith, M., *The State of Africa* (London: Simon & Schuster, 2006).

Leone which helped to end conflicts. But we should also note the special conditions of those two cases. In Mozambique, the intervention was to keep the peace; but there was a peace to keep, both belligerents being exhausted and eager for a resolution. In Sierra Leone, decisive military action against a deeply unpopular movement was followed by a virtual occupation of a relatively small country by a plethora of outside agencies. Most humanitarian interventions are nothing like as clear-cut or manageable as these, which is why we might ask whether interventions sometimes do more harm than good.

The immediate motive for humanitarian intervention is a compelling need to save lives. But urgency can impede reflection. Our urge to intervene may be impelled by our own concerns or priorities, or our deepest notions of right and wrong. But our priorities, concerns or morality may not be shared by those for whom the help is intended. Sometimes our motives may not be as noble as we like to think. We may wish to strike out at those who have offended us. Sometimes motives may be muddled. Just as development agencies must 'do projects', so humanitarian agencies must 'do disasters'. The sometimes unseemly competition for donations lends itself to exaggerated claims. Beyond these complexities the sense of urgency – the need to 'do something' – fosters two beguiling simplifications. The first is a reluctance to analyse the situation, since reflection might prompt delay. The second is a reluctance to think through the goals of intervention, the means required to attain them, and the realistic chances of success. Because the urge to 'do something' can be satisfied by doing anything, the hard-headed assessment of what may actually be possible can be postponed.

If we are sceptical about the promoters of humanitarian intervention, there is no less basis for being sceptical about its supposed beneficiaries. There are a number of reasons to suggest that humanitarian intervention may actually do harm. The

Western intervention in Libya had ripple effects all over North Africa and the Sahel states and led to major upheavals in a number of countries, notably Mali. Interventions that are supposed to be politically neutral increasingly choose to identify with one party against another, or are successfully manipulated into such a position. Outside forces now increasingly tend to make ethical or legal judgments about different military and political actors, often reducing a complex narrative to 'good' guys and 'bad' guys. This tends to obscure other kinds of violence which may not fit the main narrative. The violence of the Lord's Resistance Army (LRA), a guerrilla group operating in the north of Uganda, is notorious, and in reaction the US supported counter-insurgency campaigns. The violence of the Ugandan army in northern Uganda, on the other hand, is much less well known, and Uganda has continued to be a 'donor darling'. This, in turn, makes it much more likely that the potential for violence in the future will be ignored.

Becoming aligned with one party may reinforce the dominant group, or relieve the pressure to compromise. Even in the absence of such alignments, the sheer presence of outside intervening forces provides almost endless possibilities for the diversion of resources. It was humanitarian aid that the outside world delivered to Somalia in the 1990s. Within months of that intervention it became clear that the various rival clans and groups were stealing food aid and using it to continue their battles. There are many other ways intervention can assist conflicting groups. Humanitarian sanctuaries can serve insurgents as buffer zones or enable them to recruit fighters. The ration cards that are used to distribute humanitarian aid by the UN agencies are forged or stolen to provide access to supplies. Insurgent groups may even drive refugees into areas they control so as to acquire such supplies. Armed factions can loot food, medicines, communications equipment, and vehicles from aid organisations, as they did in Liberia. They can attack refugee camps, killing and abducting inhabitants and looting supplies, as they did in Sierra Leone.

It could of course be argued that such losses, while regrettable, should not be allowed to undermine the importance of intervention itself. But rather than simply stealing what is already there, armed groups may deliberately engage in conflict, even atrocities, in order to attract attention or to bid up their price for participating in peace-making or conflict resolution. These groups have become more adept at playing the game, rapidly mastering what agendas and political phraseology appeals to outside actors. Nor are these tendencies restricted to insurgent groups. African governments that have encountered political opposition now rush to accuse them of atrocities or terrorism in order to secure a sympathetic international hearing or material support. They have levied taxes or charges on NGOs bringing resources to conflict areas. They have used control of aid resources to build alliances or control civilian populations.

The record of humanitarian intervention in African conflicts provides much evidence to sustain scepticism about its purposes and effects. The largest humanitarian intervention in modern times has been deployed in the Democratic Republic of the Congo. The UN mission in that country has a budget of $1.5 billion a year and a military and police force of some 20,000 personnel. Donors have poured billions more into development and democracy-related projects in the last two decades. An enormous country, about the size of Western Europe, it was probably the worst governed state in Africa under its long-time President Mobutu, overthrown in a rebellion in 1997. It has been embroiled in conflict virtually ever since, particularly in its eastern regions, which are themselves about the size of France.

The nature of these conflicts is extraordinarily complex (there are some thirty to forty warring groups), but Western intervention has been shaped by a handful of factors. The first is the widespread assumption that the conflict is being driven by competition for natural resources, whether by direct control of mines or 'taxing' those who work in them. One of the worst effects of the conflict that has mobilised Western engagement is the widespread sexual abuse of women. The response to both these issues has been to restore the power and authority of the central state. This has been the central purpose behind the UN intervention force (MONUC, later MONUSCO) established in 1999, whose mandate has been steadily expanded ever since so that the mission is now involved in the full range of 'peace-building', which includes consolidating democracy, promoting good governance, protecting human rights, and engaging with civil society.

On virtually all counts it is fair to say the mission has failed: partly because MONUSCO has nothing like sufficient resources, nor is it ever likely to have; partly because the standardised approach to 'state-building' neglects the specific conditions in each state and partly because many of the powerful political actors in DRC have little interest in establishing a proper state. Rather they have an interest in maintaining the facade of a state, giving them access to resources and donor funds, but at the same time leaving the state weak so they can engage in illicit economic activities and preserve the ultimate insurance of the armed groups under their command. Continued conflict, provided it does not get out of hand, is actually good for business. As Moise Katumbi, one-time governor of Katanga, the largest province, put it, the political class 'think the country is a cow that you milk but don't feed'.[*]

So not only does Western engagement do little on its own terms, it has actually made things worse. As one authority on the Congo suggests:

---

[*] Pilling, D., 'Is trucking tycoon Moise Katumbi the man to rescue Congo?', *Financial Times*, 7 July 2017.

the international efforts have exacerbated the problems that they aimed to combat: the attempts to control the exploitation of resources have enabled armed groups to strengthen their control over mines; the disproportionate attention to sexual violence has raised the status of sexual abuse to an effective bargaining tool for combatants; and the state reconstruction programmes have boosted the capacity of an authoritarian regime to oppress its population.*

There is one further reason why all this effort is undermined. Two regional powers, Uganda and Rwanda, while they have rather different agendas, both find it useful and profitable to meddle in the political situation in eastern DRC to the extent of supporting various militias, even (almost certainly) deploying their own troops across the border. These countries, too, are 'donor darlings' and receive substantial amounts of foreign aid. While there are occasional rebukes, even occasional suspensions of aid, the flow invariably resumes, and no real attempt is made to constrain these activities.

The unfortunate effects of the Western urge to 'do good' is even more painfully evident in the case of South Sudan. Sudan, the third largest country in Africa, had been woefully neglected as a British colony, and a large part of that neglect rested in the concentration of resources in the north and the neglect of the south. Very roughly this division aligns with religion (the north is Muslim), and to some extent race and ethnicity (the north is Arab and the south is African). After independence in 1955, periods of relative stability were punctuated by northern efforts to impose a Muslim identity on the south and continued economic neglect of the region, which prompted a southern rebellion, beginning in 1983, by the Sudan People's Liberation Movement (SPLA), a conflict that was ended by the

---

* Autesserre, S., 'Dangerous tales: dominant narratives on the Congo and their unintended consequences', *African Affairs*, 111(443), 2012, pp. 202–22 at p. 205.

Comprehensive Peace Agreement in 2005. (A complication was the outbreak of conflict in the western Darfur region in 2003.)

For various reasons Sudan attracted the ire of Western opinion, and various wild accusations of genocide and even apartheid were made. President Omar al-Bashir was indicted by the ICC after referral by the UN Security Council. In these circumstances, the SPLA played its hand well, capitalising on anti-Islam sentiment and playing the part of a state in waiting, mouthing all the right words about development and democracy. The Comprehensive Peace Agreement duly included a clause allowing for a referendum on full independence for South Sudan. Held in 2011, the referendum voted overwhelmingly for independence, and there was much talk of new hope and optimism. But this optimism was rudely dashed: the West had misread the SPLA which, far from being a unified force representing the south and committed to democracy and development, was actually a fragile alliance of military chieftains with different ethnic and regional loyalties, whose main interest lay in consuming the bulk of the new state's revenue. In 2012, the new president, Salva Kiir Mayardit, acknowledged that $4 billion, probably more, had gone missing from the public accounts.* Vice President Riek Machar's announcement that he would challenge for the leadership led to an increasingly tense situation which finally erupted into violence at the end of 2013. Tens of thousands have been killed, some 5 million people need food assistance, and there is little prospect of the conflict being resolved. It is not at all clear that the foundation of a new state in South Sudan was a step forward.

---

* 'Billions of dollars had disappeared from its [Sudan's] coffers and would remain unaccounted for.' See Hemmer, J. and Grinstead, N., 'When peace is the exception: shifting the donor narrative in South Sudan', CRU Policy Brief (The Hague: Clingendael, Netherlands Institute of International Relations, 2015), p. 3.

'WE JUST HAVE TO GO THROUGH THE MOTIONS'*

If humanitarian intervention has tended to be short term and dramatic, attempts to change Africa more fundamentally have been more long term and carefully calibrated. As we have seen, one technique has been to place various kinds of external pressures and constraints on African states and leaders. While these, on occasion, looked quite fierce, and were occasionally successful, in the main these efforts signally failed, and African leaders have repeatedly shown that they can turn many of the demands placed on them to their advantage. Consider one of the main demands: that African states privatise large sections of their economies. These pressures were driven by developments in our own societies, as much as anything else. Throughout the Western world, starting in the 1980s but continuing since then, the idea has been vociferously promoted that 'the market' was not just the only way to run the productive economy, but the best way to run utilities such as water and energy, often seen even in the West as natural monopolies best run by the state in the public interest. But it is not hard to see how such ideas seemed peculiarly appropriate to the Africa of the time. Because African states controlled so much of their countries' economies, and in so doing had accumulated unsustainable levels of debt, and because those economies had been so spectacularly unsuccessful, the arguments for privatisation seemed even more compelling than elsewhere. On the one hand, measures to reduce state involvement in the economy would cut out inefficiency and waste, minimise opportunities for corruption, and reduce public sector debt. On the other hand, promoting a market economy would encourage entrepreneurship, attract more investment, bring in new technology and revive economic growth.

---

* The view of an Ugandan government official from Lie, J. H. S., *Developmentality: An Ethnography of the World Bank-Uganda Partnership* (New York: Berghahn Books, 2015), p. 172.

There was of course something to be said for these arguments. The state sectors and public utilities of many African economies were often extremely badly run, either because of corruption or incompetence, or both. African states did subsidise many loss-making enterprises and often had little idea of how to resolve their fundamental difficulties. It is even fair to say that, on occasion, privatisation of such enterprises worked, a much-quoted example being Kenya Airways, once a basket case, and now generally agreed to be one of the best airlines in Africa. In line with this thinking, the World Bank and the IMF pushed countries very hard to privatise state-owned enterprises (SOEs), often making privatisation a condition of other kinds of economic and financial support. In the 1990s, Zambia was forced to privatise large sections of its economy on pain of losing debt relief. However, such measures almost nowhere had the effects so fondly anticipated. Not only did they not lead to an explosion of entrepreneurial activity, but also many of the businesses or businesspeople that took over state companies were incapable of running these companies effectively. Some Zambian mines were bought by new private owners simply to strip and sell off existing machinery or other assets. Agreements they had entered into with African governments were often not honoured. Obligations to workforces were abandoned. And this was, according to the World Bank, the most successful privatisation programme in Africa!

Ironically, one of the very promises that made privatisation attractive in Africa – that it would reduce corruption – almost everywhere had the opposite effect. Far from being analogous to the successes of Eastern Europe after the Cold War, these priva-tisations were more akin to the disastrous transition of Russia to capitalism, which gave birth to the oligarchs. All over Africa, presidents and their allies seized the opportunity to reinforce their own political networks and undermine their political oppo-nents. Nor were they the only ones to make privatisation benefit themselves. Army officers and state officials pressed for privatisation policies for entirely self-interested reasons. The very large funds made available by the international financial institutions for state sector reform gave African leaders an opportunity to sell public assets to political friends and businesspeople on highly favourable, and often highly dubious, terms. Such terms included disposal without tendering, the withholding of information, distorting prices, putting confidants on the boards of companies, and allowing protracted repayment periods. In Zambia, state farms were sold off to ex-finance ministers. The revenue from some privatisations simply disappeared. Many of these sales included state enterprises which had been 'rehabilitated' with aid money. The harm was compounded by the obsession of the IMF and the World Bank with very rapid privatisation.

Nor was the experience of utility privatisation any more reassuring. For a period, Western states and international organisations demanded that African states privatise utilities, and huge financial resources were made available to make the policy a success. Such resources often benefited large Western corporations that secured the bulk of such contracts. There is little evidence that the privatisation of water supplies has improved service delivery. Competition has not worked, there is little evidence that private operators are more efficient, or that they have improved investment in water infrastructure. At least a third of such contracts have been cancelled by African governments, having failed to deliver what they promised.

The International Criminal Court, too, which had been designed as a universal means of conflict resolution and deterrence of corruption, was not used elsewhere in the world. At the time of its conception in the late 1990s, and its coming into existence after being ratified by sixty countries, it seemed peculiarly suited to deal with African issues. Africa was an area of considerable conflict, much of that conflict 'barbaric' and aimed against civilians. As a result, at the time of writing, the ICC has only engaged in cases in Africa. On the face of it this seems implausible. Is Africa the only place in the world where 'crimes against humanity' and 'war crimes' are committed? Moreover, this particular form of external meddling is sometimes more damaging than others. We might start by noting that Robin Cook, British foreign secretary in Blair's Labour government, famously said that the ICC was 'not a court set up to bring to book prime ministers of the United Kingdom or presidents of the United States'. Exactly so. Powerful states can ignore the ICC, since it needs their support to function at all. Those same powerful states can also protect friendly states and undermine unfriendly ones. Weak states, on the other hand, will attract the attention of the ICC, which desperately needs to prove itself as an effective international actor. Unfortunately, it is often difficult to deter conflict and secure justice at the same time: there is often a trade-off, largely because most modern conflicts are within, rather than between, states. Certainly in Africa, although states and armed movements occasionally intervene across borders, the conflict dynamics are overwhelmingly internal, and often between 'civilians', which is one of the reasons why the distinction between 'combatant' and 'non-combatant' is not particularly useful in making sense of such conflicts. Resolution is not made easier by outsiders, or even insiders, labelling some conflict parties as 'criminals' and demanding that they be brought to justice, when these are the very people who must be involved in any agreement to make peace.

Beyond the peace versus justice dilemma, the promoters of the ICC persistently overlook the fact that local actors have their own agendas. Both African governments and the leaders of opposition movements have been quick to assess that the ICC presents some rather attractive opportunities. A prestigious international organisation, supported by some of the world's richest and most powerful states, armed with powers to investigate, indict and issue arrest warrants, whose personnel are eager to demonstrate their importance and competence, can be quite a useful ally in internal political battles. This explains why some of the African cases the ICC has pursued, as its promoters never cease to proclaim, were a result of 'invitation' by African states. Indeed, the very first case in which the Court issued arrest warrants resulted from an invitation by Uganda's President Museveni for the ICC to involve itself in the campaign against the Lord's Resistance Army. Noted for its vicious tactics and lack of political programme, this group attracted considerable notoriety and international disapproval, and the Ugandan government had signally failed to repress it by military means. Inviting the ICC to take up the issue gave Museveni considerable political cover and international legitimacy, significant gains for a government dependent on foreign aid. Whatever its faults, the LRA is rooted in a history of violent conflict in the region in which the Ugandan Army has also been a participant. For the ICC, which had in fact connived at the 'invitation' before it was delivered, successful prosecutions seemed likely to garner international credibility and prestige. But its openly partisan approach (the ICC prosecutor shared platforms with the Ugandan president before there had been any investigations), which meant turning a blind eye to the repression of the Ugandan government and its own army, not only did not end the conflict or provide a deterrent, but arguably obstructed the process of resolving it.

But of course two can play that game. One of the reasons that the LRA proved so difficult to deal with was that it had received support from the government of Sudan, which had not forgotten that Uganda had given support to the SPLA in its struggle for an independent South Sudan. It was the old story of 'my enemy's enemy is my friend'. In the case of Sudan, it was the major Western powers, through the UN Security Council, that orchestrated sanctions and arrest warrants for two Sudanese government officials, and later for the Sudanese president himself. What prompted these moves was the violent conflict in Darfur, which attracted intense Western disapproval of Sudan's attempts to crush insurgencies. Not surprisingly, the leaders of these movements enthusiastically welcomed ICC involvement and made much of the contrast between themselves and the Sudanese government. Despite their mouthing of lofty platitudes of 'international justice', these leaders' interest in the ICC was primarily to brand their opponents as international criminals, and thereby gain legitimacy. But when political circumstances changed, and their military position weakened, they were happy to agree an amnesty with the Sudanese government which completely ignored international law and the ICC.

The Sudanese case might even give pause for thought to those who favour an international criminal court. Despite the arrest warrant issued against President al-Bashir, he has travelled widely in Africa and the Middle East, including countries that are signatories to the Rome Treaty, and none of these states have been prepared to arrest him. The UN Security Council, which triggered the whole process, has neither proposed sanctions, nor even verbally rebuked these states.

'WE DON'T ASK THE EUROPEANS TO BE POLY-GAMISTS'

Notions of democracy and human rights are deeply embedded in the political culture of the West, having acquired the status of almost religious truth. Even to question their appropriateness at certain times in certain places, and in certain circumstances, provokes extreme suspicion. Yet this dogmatic certainty, while perfectly understandable as a political tactic, is relatively recent and not very persuasive. To make only the most obvious point here: there are huge differences of opinion in the West about democracy, regarding its institutional forms (different kinds of voting systems, different legislative procedures), its scope (ideas like 'economic' democracy, 'deliberative' democracy) and its more theoretical justifications (is it more about representation or participation?). The forms of democracy in Western states are the outcome of these debates, as well as national histories and experiences, over quite long periods of historical time. So American democracy looks rather different from British or French democracy.

The situation in Africa presents a dramatic contrast. Before 1991, virtually every state in Africa, with the remarkable exception of Botswana, took a more or less authoritarian form. No government in Africa had ever been replaced as a result of an election – including in Botswana. In 1991, Cape Verde, Benin and Zambia broke the mould and instituted multiparty politics. Since then, virtually every African state has followed suit. Military coups occasionally still occur, but these invariably prove temporary. Multiparty politics looks set to stay in Africa – surely an unqualified sign of progress?

As we have had occasion to note several times in this book it is a mistake to imagine that African ruling elites simply adopt what is urged on them in terms of 'international norms', and they may well have their own reasons for moving in a certain direction. This certainly applies to democracy. The sheer rapidity of adoption of multiparty democracy suggests this was in part for external consumption. As one French scholar, Jean-François Bayart, has somewhat mischievously suggested, Senegal's biggest export is democracy. In one or two cases this is indisputable. The Nyalali Commission, set up in 1990 in Tanzania to explore the desire for multiparty democracy, found that a majority of Tanzanians expressed a wish to retain the one-party system. Tanzania adopted multiparty democracy in 1992 anyway. One of the most striking things about democracy in Africa is how uniform it is. Almost everywhere, elites have set up what political scientists call presidential regimes; no longer, it is true, run by the unfettered autocrats of old, but still concentrating enormous power, including huge financial powers, in their hands. There is little interest in adapting the wide range of possible democratic forms to African circumstances. European democracy is far more varied. To be fair, more recently Western commentary has become more sceptical in its account of African democracy, spawning a new vocabulary of 'democracy with adjectives', such as 'low-intensity democracy', 'hybrid democracy', or 'competitive authoritarianism'. So it is not unreasonable to suggest that, while the formalities of elections are now well established, the continued 'democratisation' of African societies is by no means certain and novel forms of rule may emerge.

African leaders may well have other reasons for adopting democracy. Winning elections contributes to the prestige of the ruling party and undermines that of its opponents. Western pressure for democracy has brought in its wake fairly generous funding, much of which can be used for patronage. Sometimes multiparty democracy provides a way of overcoming or marginalising opposition by enforcing party discipline. In some ways, the Ugandan parliament functioned more effectively without formal political parties; and one of the reasons that President Museveni adopted multiparty democracy, apart from to please the donors, was to impose tighter control on his supporters. President Biya in Cameroon, one of Africa's longest serving rulers, has proved adept at manipulating the rules of electoral registration, as well as the idea of minority cultural rights, to enhance his party's control of power. Many regimes in Africa have used the legitimacy of winning elections to close down or restrict the political space of their opponents, or to restrict the media. Election campaigns are expensive and drive corruption as politicians struggle to find the resources to wage them. Is it any coincidence that the biggest corruption scandals in Kenya have occurred since the adoption of multiparty democracy? To win elections, parties must mobilise voters to go and vote. Most people in all democracies vote on vague instincts. In countries where people are not fundamentally at loggerheads, identities remain largely political; but in countries where there are distinct communities with different ethnic, religious and regional ties, the mobilisation of such identities can become antagonistic – even violent. These considerations apply equally to decentralisation, some form of which has been adopted by virtually every African state. There is next to no evidence that poverty indicators have improved as result of decentralisation, or that it has benefited the poor. Nor is there much evidence that it has made African societies more democratic. Rather, almost everywhere in Africa, decentralisation has been essentially used to consolidate alliances between the central state and local elites, reinforcing central power. It has tended to fuel identity politics at the local level because that largely determines who has access to resources. That, in turn, has prompted struggles between local elites and between different ethnic groups.

Even if most people, on reflection, might be persuaded that democracy can take various forms depending on its wider social context, far fewer are likely to be persuaded that the same might be said of human rights. Human rights have always been presented as compelling, universal, brooking no exceptions. It is not hard to see why such language would appeal in Africa, where so many have experienced the indignities and cruelties of political repression. As with democracy, the blunt assertion of human rights as simply 'universal' obscures the many ways rights can be understood and implemented. Part of the difficulty here is that rights can be understood in narrower or broader senses. The narrowest sense aims to place limitations on the power of the state to harm citizens, conferring the right not to be tortured, not to be imprisoned without trial, and political rights. Even in this sense there are some acknowledged circumstances in which they may be overridden or in conflict. When rights are understood in the broadest sense, a whole new set of contradictions becomes apparent. 'Rights talk' has insinuated itself into more and more areas of life: the rights agenda goes way beyond its original concerns and now makes huge claims as to how human societies should function and human beings should behave in virtually every sphere of life. One of the more obvious tensions is between individual and cultural rights. Both of these are defined in various human rights documents, but the tensions between them are resolved in the West by a sometimes explicit, but often tacit assumption that individual rights override cultural rights. This is not a universal assumption.

Consider the case of Mali, widely regarded by Western opinion, after decades of high levels of aid, as a flagship democracy, until a military coup in 2012. The country's successive constitutions all embodied Western liberal assumptions about gender equality, but these hardly reflected actual practice. Even marriage law itself allowed for polygamous marriage. In practice, the institution of marriage in Mali was a mix of secular principles, Islamic legal norms and deference to 'custom'. Many marriages were never registered with the state, though they were governed by Islamic norms. Ever since independence, some women's groups in Mali have been calling for reform, which the Mali government ostensibly accepted. At the same time, many Muslim associations also wanted to see the state acknowledge Islamic marriages. In 2009, the government presented a bill to parliament that would 'modernise' the marriage law to bring it into line with Western norms. The Mali government, mindful of its dependence on donor aid and Western lobbies, placed heavy pressure on MPs to pass the bill, which they did almost unanimously, even though it clearly deviated from local practice. When it became public knowledge, it generated the largest protest demonstration in the country in twenty years, and opposition to the law was increasingly cast in terms of an attack, encouraged by the West, on Malian traditions. The proposed law was hastily withdrawn. It is frequently argued that African countries have bound themselves by various agreements, including the Maputo Protocol (guaranteeing gender equality).

It is true that many such agreements have been signed, but it is also true that many leaders know that these paper commitments bear no relation to the real-world conditions in their societies.

But dogmatic applications of 'rights' can do damage well beyond the intimate sphere of life where the gap between the West and Africa is at its most acute. In 2006, Botswana's high court issued its judgment in the case of Sesana v The Attorney General. The case was the longest and most expensive in the country's history. The dispute concerned the relocation of 'indigenous' San people from the Central Kalahari Game Reserve (CKGR), a large area of land originally declared a nature reserve by the colonial government, allowing some continuing settlement by 'Bushmen'. The Bushmen or San are probably one of the most studied people in the world; indeed, the creation of the reserve had been partly a result of the intense public interest sparked by the books of author Laurens van der Post.* They are, or rather were, in the anthropological jargon, 'hunter-gatherers', and the West, as with many other such 'primitive' people, has veered between its impulses to modernise and to preserve their culture. The Botswana government decided that these people should be moved into settlements where better facilities could be provided for them. Whatever the rights and wrongs of this decision, the government found its policy blocked by new ideological trends in the West that only really gathered momentum in the 1970s, prompting increasing demands for recognition of the rights of 'indigenous' peoples. Such demands were backed by funding from Western states and private organisations. In the San case, the Botswana government had been pursuing negotiations with the Bushmen, and many had in fact moved to areas with better welfare services. But the dispute turned sour when the British NGO Survival International (originally known

---

* The famous South African explorer and writer also produced a popular TV series, *Lost World of the Kalahari*.

as the Primitive People's Fund) insisted on pursuing land rights
for the San within the reserve by means of an aggressive policy
of international campaigning, involving boycotts and celebrity
denunciations, accusing the Botswana government of trafficking
in 'blood diamonds' and 'genocide'. Although the court's decision
required the Botswana government to allow the Bushmen to
return, it has interpreted the decision very narrowly, and in a
sense the situation remains unresolved. The Botswana government's anger at some aspects of the case seem entirely
understandable. Nowhere in the world has 'development' been
without costs, and it is not at all clear that any other agency has
a better claim to decide on development in Botswana. The case
suggests also that African states have had good reason to be
sceptical about the idea of 'indigenous peoples' in Africa, an
idea which may make sense in circumstances of clear historical
conquest, but may threaten disunity and division in Africa for
no great gain.

The democracy and human rights agendas are not the magic
bullets they are so often claimed to be. Rights agendas give
Western states and NGOs extraordinary access to African societies to promote 'universal' norms, which are anything but. Their
superior resources give them considerable leverage over domestic
African organisations, but they have no accountability to people
in those societies (and very little to people in their own societies). Needless to say, African organisations would never be
allowed such access to Western societies. Far from resolving
social and political tensions, rights agendas actually exacerbate
them. Rights claims become entrenched and resistant to compromise. Even in long-established homogeneous societies this can
be problematic (think of disputes about abortion, for example);
but in highly fractured societies it can be disastrous.

Lastly, these reflections suggest that 'rights' and 'democracy'
do not necessarily point in the same direction, and that the
relationship between them is tricky. It more or less works in the

West because the term 'rights' marks a space where there is a consensus on certain basic values, and the term 'democracy' marks a space where decisions can be made on the basis of majority voting. In societies where this demarcation is by no means established, democracy and rights may well clash, impeding the pragmatic management of social tensions. The aggressive promotion of rights, in deference to outside demands, threatens to discredit democracy. Equally, the aggressive promotion of democracy is likely to provoke antagonism in highly divided societies. Given the subtleties and complexities of social change in African societies, only the most boundless arrogance could imagine that meaningful social change could be brought about in this way by outsiders. Stung by Western complaints about African attitudes, President Macky Sall of Senegal snapped: 'We don't ask the Europeans to be polygamists. We like polygamy in our country, but we can't impose it in yours.'* Europeans show little in the way of such restraint. In the following chapter I suggest they might learn something from Africa.

---

* 'Senegalese president defends anti-gay law', *CBS News* [online], 28 June 2013. Retrieved from https://www.cbsnews.com/news/senegalese-president-defends-anti-gay-law/

8

CHANGING DIRECTION

'WE SAY ALL KINDS OF THINGS TO PLEASE THE IMF'*

T HE CASE AGAINST THE WESTERN PROJECT in Africa seems overwhelming. Why then does it continue? The guilt story remains powerful and drives the idea that the solutions to Africa's problems are to be found, and funded, by outsiders. Vacillating between indulgent and punitive, these solutions have come to rest more and more on a sense of superiority – a conviction that 'we' are always right. Our economic practices, our political institutions, our values must be adopted. Their practices, cultures and traditions must be abandoned or eradicated. Power and conviction are never far from arrogance. Whatever it is that currently bothers us (the environment, feminism, the aged, the young, disability) must immediately be taken up by 'them'.

With superiority and arrogance comes a kind of strategic

* A Maasai schoolteacher quoted in Archambault, Caroline, 'Pain with punishment and the negotiation of childhood: An ethnographic analysis of children's rights processes in Maasailand', *Africa*, 79.2, 2009, p. 298.

blindness which enables us to avoid awkward questions. The evidence of the negative effects of our engagement with Africa is ignored; we apply all sorts of double standards without any kind of explanation; we do not ask any hard questions about our own failings (after all, we are generous with aid); we reduce complex questions until they are crude appeals to guilt or sympathy; we rely on fads and buzzwords. But this sense of power, of knowing what is best for others and always doing good, is haunted by a sense of failure, even impotence. How is it possible, if we are so superior, for us to fail?

So many policies have been tried, reinvented, and tried again. Poverty reduction was centre stage in 1973, in 1990, and again in 2001. Nothing seems to work. There are now more poor people in Africa than there were. From time to time we find ourselves overwhelmed by 'aid fatigue'. The disparity between our slogans and our actual capabilities seems huge, even daunting. Aid budgets climb relentlessly upwards, but are never sufficient.* We intervene to prevent conflicts, only to make them worse. Endless rounds of negotiations to end conflicts produce no result. We scour every nook and cranny of African societies, but can't figure out what makes them tick. One year Africa is rising, the next year it is not. Mali was a 'donor darling' and a successful, stable democracy until 2012, when it suddenly became a 'fragile state' – an 'ungoverned space'.

And how is it that Africa's leaders, who once spoke the language of pan-Africanism and promised the death of tribalism, rapid progress and 'jet-propelled' social change, have also demanded the continuation of the Western project? As the dreams of independence encountered the tough realities of bad luck and the steep learning

---

* In 1973, Robert McNamara, then President of the World Bank, called for a doubling of aid. In 2001, one of his successors, James Wolfenson, called for another doubling. Gordon Brown, British Chancellor of the Exchequer, demanded the doubling of British aid in 2002, and was as good as his word.

curves of effective ruling while growing and changing, what had once been seen as a temporary lifeline became a kind of life support. For two generations, a significant portion of these resources has been provided by others as a gift. But material dependence threatens subservience: 'There can be nothing more humiliating for a government representative to go cap in hand begging for assistance from donors', says the Tanzanian minister of finance.* It becomes a kind of pleading. It requires endless gratitude and constant reminders to the giver to keep giving. It is also a constant pressure to emulate the giver, to take the advice, to follow the guide. This erodes self-belief. It is a kind of disabling, a reluctance to confront realities and do something about them. In a state of dependence it is easy to propose another project, agree another treaty, issue another statement, have another round of negotiations.

For decades, African leaders have issued ringing declarations about 'self-sufficiency', 'African solutions', 'self-reliance', 'increasing continental integration', but nothing much actually happens, and the little that does is paid for by outsiders. Constitutions and treaties are copied or imitated, but often ignored; political structures are created on paper, but not taken seriously; grandiose plans arc announccd with no clear idea as to how they are to be achieved. Dependence is also haunted by an angry twin – resentment. There are anxieties about lack of respect. However polite and friendly the dispensers of aid are (and often they are not), there seems to be no end to the issues on which advice and guidance must be accepted. This prompts a further anxiety, of a permanently subordinate position, a permanent inadequacy. The anxiety and the subordination seem inexplicable. They never seem to end. If 'they' are the experts, why haven't the problems been solved? Since 'they' are the source of aid, and it is not working, it must surely be their fault? Anger generates suspicion.

* Rwegayura, A., 'Tanzania: citizens are finally paying taxes for the good of the country', *Deutsche Welle*, on AllAfrica.com [Online], 20 July 2017. Retrieved from http://allafrica.com/stories/201707200724.html

Perhaps the aid is bogus, never really meant to help solve problems; or worse – intended to entrench continued weakness and subordination. With anger and suspicion comes, finally, the urge to strike back: to denounce, to blame, and then to demand recompense; to call the flow of resources something which restores dignity: not assistance or gifts, but entitlement – restitution.

For some sixty years, these attitudes have been locked in a mutual embrace, the inevitable by-product of which is extraordinarily high levels of mutual deception. There is the fake documentation, the false statistics, the 'ghost' employees, schools and soldiers, the pointless workshops and attendance fees. Even fake government departments. The Somali government in 2005 had a 'minister of tourism' in a country racked by violent political conflict (along with eighty other ministers). There is the extraction of extra revenue from agencies by means of 'taxes', permits or visas. There is the diversion of resources to cronies, privatisation schemes to enrich the already wealthy, decentralisation plans to tighten central political control, the anti-corruption commissions that ignore corruption. There is the agreement with, even flattery of, donors, with the clear intent of reneging on such agreement wherever possible. There is the non-repayment of loans, the non-reform of policies, the dragging out of negotiations. African presidents, like Armando Guebuza of Mozambique, make speeches solemnly affirming that 'we must start with the few resources we have instead of holding out our hand begging without even trying,'* but continue to hold out their hand. There are the insistent demands for funds to support 'peace-making', but a complete inability to enforce any peace or even, in many cases, to agree a common policy. There are the ratifications of so-called 'international norms' that are entirely at variance with the practices of African societies.

---

* Quoted in Hanlon, J. and Smart, T., *Do Bicycles Equal Development in Mozambique?* (Oxford: James Currey, 2008).

Such doublethink is not lacking in the West, even if it tends more towards self-deception. Western governments, international organisations and NGOs endlessly exaggerate. Here are a few statements from the World Bank:

- 1981: 'Policy action and foreign assistance...will surely work together to build a continent that shows real gains in both development and income in the near future.'
- 1984: 'This optimism can be justified by recent experience in Africa...some countries are introducing policy and institutional reforms.'
- 1986: 'Progress is clearly under way. Especially in the past two years, more countries have started to act, and the changes they are making go deeper than before.'
- 1989: 'Since the mid-1980s Africa has seen important changes in policies and in economic performance.'
- 1994: 'African countries have made great strides in improving policies and restoring growth.'
- 2000: 'Since the mid-1990s, there have been signs that better economic management has started to pay off.'
- 2002: 'Africa's leaders...have recognised the need to improve their policies, spelled out in the New Partnership for African Development.'

With the World Bank, things have always been improving. NGOs exaggerate all sorts of statistics in order to obtain grants and contracts. The figure of 5.4 million deaths resulting from conflict in the Congo was widely proclaimed as fact. Later estimates placed it at less than a million.* Governments and NGOs downplay the fact that vast amounts of aid go missing. On all sides the need to justify vast sums of foreign aid encourages the proliferation of buzzwords and clichés ('make poverty history', 'drop the debt', 'sustainable development')

---

* There are considerable difficulties with any such estimates.

whose plausibility is supported only by the bright smiles of entertainers. Governments and NGOs alike trumpet the virtues of
committing 0.7% of GDP to aid without evidence or explanation.
Western governments have asserted that foreign aid and intervention
will halt wars, prevent migration, and even benefit Western economies. Dubious assertions are often joined by dubious facts. The
attacks on Libya in 2011 were justified by assertions that the Libyan
government was about to engage in massive revenge killing of civilians, for which there was little evidence. The absurdities and
contradictions of various conditionalities are routinely ignored. The
defence budget of Burundi, by virtue of the country's participation
in peace-keeping missions in Somalia, is almost completely supplied
by donors. The money goes direct to the government, not the
soldiers, though they are still well paid. When President Pierre
Nkurunziza announced his intention to stand for a third term, this
sparked opposition and a full-scale political crisis, fairly brutally
suppressed by soldiers. The West dutifully denounced the repression,
carried out by an army that it was financing. In Somalia, Kenyan
Defence Forces, part of the UN African Union Mission in Somalia
(AMISOM), funded by international donors, collude with the very
enemy they are supposed to be fighting, Al-Shabaab, in the smug-
gling of charcoal and sugar out of the country.

These are only some of the cruder forms of deception. It is
perfectly possible for the donors to deceive, even impede each
other. Donor governments (the 'bilateral donors') can find themselves being undermined by the multilateral institutions.
Sometimes the multilateral institutions are undermined by
groups of bilateral donors. The absurdities of these situations
are readily apparent. The multilateral agencies do not have secret
pots of money – their resources come from member governments. So, in the curious world of aid, donor governments and
their taxpayers can finance organisations which overtly or
covertly undermine their own purposes. Such situations can
even involve officials of the same government in mutual decep-

tion. Sir Edward Clay, a British high commissioner to Kenya, (2001–5), made it his business to investigate and publicise the massive and systemic corruption at the heart of the Kenyan government, corruption which he denounced in a speech in 2004, saying that 'it is outrageous to think that corruption accounts here and now in Kenya for about 8% of Kenya's GDP'. But as he did so, he found his position increasingly undermined by DFID officials determined to block his efforts. In this they were eminently successful. Between 2002 and 2006, British aid to Kenya nearly trebled. Perhaps the most ingenious forms of deception are those where both parties collude in it. We know they are going to break the rules and we do nothing about it. We connive in them blaming us for certain things provided they do other things we ask. They know we have to spend the 0.7% GDP, and that we have to claim this spending has been successful.

ENDING THE WESTERN PROJECT

This whole cluster of attitudes and practices has had disastrous effects and it is high time it was abandoned. The idea that 'we' – British people, Americans, Europeans, 'the West' – perhaps even 'white' people – are somehow peculiarly malevolent, responsible for all the ills of the world, and therefore must forever apologise for our sins and make amends, continues to be powerful. It lies behind the current fashion for apologising for historical events, like the Irish potato famine or the slave trade. But it is absurd. In reality, the capacities for aggression and domination, for greed and exploitation are clearly universal, and we can find them in, and between, virtually every known human society. The ills of the present will not be alleviated by an obsession with the ills of the past; nor will the problems that some human societies face today be resolved through endless begging.

We should of course face up to historical realities of all kinds, not just the few which are selected to drive contemporary political agendas. Western domination of the world, fairly well established by the late eighteenth century, certainly by the middle of the nineteenth, is the most recent historical memory of virtually all human societies. That domination took its most concrete form in machines of war, the artillery, the battleships, and later missiles and drones, that could overwhelm all resistance. But it also affected the world of ideas. The ideas of the powerful tend to be powerful ideas. So large parts of the non-Western world were not just conquered by force of arms but were also won over to new ideas, even if only because mastery of those ideas seemed an essential part of resisting conquest and domination.

There is an often unstated assumption that Western culture, Western ways of doing things, Western societies, have proven their superiority over others. True, this is no longer expressed in the arrogant terms of 'standard of civilisation', but despite fairly ritualistic assertions of equality, and a somewhat contrived tolerance of cultural variety, it is plain that so-called 'international norms' are of Western provenance, and that they must prevail. Islamic punishments are 'barbaric', African family practices are 'backward'. Such attitudes of superiority make us somehow godlike, able to judge and entitled to instruct others, even admonish them. At the limit, they seem to give us the right to smite the wicked or, in contemporary versions of that language, to punish 'human rights abusers'; to seek out the evil men who have made the world impure and bring them to (our) justice. We need to abandon this superiority complex, the idea that the only way is our way, that whatever they do can only be an inadequate form of what they should do, which is to be like us.

Abandoning these attitudes clears the ground, but they need replacing with a different and better set of orientations. What we most need is a sense of realism. The word 'realism' often has rather dreary overtones of mean-spiritedness and complacency, but it need not be so. But what realism is needed? The first is ethical realism about what kinds of moral obligations we find compelling. Much thinking in the Western tradition insists that such obligations, whatever they might be, are universal. They apply to all people irrespective of place, time and belonging. But this is deeply implausible. The fact of the matter is that the vast majority of people feel strong moral obligations towards their family, then their immediate community and, on the largest scale, their country. However much philosophers and moralists may deplore this, it is what makes it possible for most people to acknowledge that a variety of moral obligations may exist in the world, none of which is universally compelling. This idea is the basis of tolerance for different religious traditions, for example. Neither of these two facts is incompatible with a third – namely, an ethics of solidarity. There is plentiful evidence that while most people place limits on the extent of their moral obligations, they acknowledge, beyond the bounds of language, culture and society, the needs of others, including, on occasion, the need for help. After all, we never know when we might need help.

We also need to be realistic about international politics. We live in a world of states. The whole of the earth's land surface is claimed by states (with the exception of Antarctica), and states also claim territorial waters and the air space above their territory. States are rather peculiar. On the one hand, they are obviously extremely unequal; some are more powerful than others, some are more productive, have larger populations than others, and so on. On the other hand, states are in some senses equal. Only states can be members of the United Nations; only states can participate in international treaties; only states can 'recognise' other states, and so on. This distinction has brought about two different kinds of relations between states. One consists of individual agreements or conflicts, pursued on a calculation of interest. Ultimately such matters have been determined by power and war. The second consists of attempts by states to establish more general agreements that all states should abide by. Such agreements also have an element of self-interest, but they are generally argued to be in the common interest. Arguments about international politics largely turn on how each of these spheres should be managed, the sphere of power (the rules of war, diplomacy), and the sphere of agreement ('norms', treaties, international law), and which of them should predominate.

This structure of international politics has been largely devised and regulated by Western powers, and it is quite possible that new developments may change it. While the Western world remains the global economic powerhouse, and the United States the largest single economy, economic activity and power is clearly shifting towards newly industrialising countries, especially China. There are also cultural shifts that might undermine Western predominance, most notably the revival of Islam as a political project. For these reasons, the field of international relations is in flux in the early twenty-first century, and we do not know where these forces and arguments will lead. What we can say is that the world of nation states is here to stay, and it is, on balance, the best way of organising a world of very different cultures and peoples. The sphere of sovereignty does not exclude cooperation and even solidarity. States cooperate in all sorts of ways that go beyond narrow self-interest. Even rich well-governed states experience natural or man-made disasters from time to time, during which they should expect the assistance of other states. Nor does respect for sovereignty preclude the view that certain states have more difficulties than others, deserve certain kinds of support more than others, and so on.

Finally, we need historical and sociological realism; a sense of what is possible over time. The difficulty here is that there is a widespread impatience in the contemporary world with the idea that social and political change takes time. People yearn for a 'new world', a magic key that will make all things wonderful at once. But the human world is not like that. Nowhere in the world has been 'turned into a paradise' in ten years, as Kwame Nkrumah once hoped. Nowhere has industrialised in ten years, as Samora Machel once promised. And the 2020 or 2025 'visions' that most African countries now have are not going to happen either. Human societies vary enormously, and all historical experience shows that changing them is a difficult business, and that the sequencing of such change is one of the greatest of those difficulties. Does productivity come before poverty? Should growth take priority over democracy? We do have vast amounts of knowledge about such processes in the historical past, and we can even make some rough and ready generalisations about that past, but such generalisations are not, as some fondly imagine, 'laws' that can be straightforwardly applied in any set of circumstances to bring about predictable results.

There are still good reasons to pursue reflection on these matters, of course. It teaches us some modesty about the appropriateness of our own experience for others. It is useful to learn from different experiences. If one is attempting to industrialise, it is still worth studying eighteenth-century Britain. But it would be extremely foolish only to study eighteenth-century Britain, and very sensible to study nineteenth-century Japan and twentieth-century Korea. Historical and sociological realism alerts us to two other important points. The first is that the context in which social and political change takes place is tremendously important. It has been, for example, a genuine difficulty for African societies that they became independent in the late twentieth century when human aspirations everywhere were at historically unprecedented levels, but so also were the technological means to fulfil them. Those same technological means, in the form of modern communications technology, have made the living standards of the prosperous world more and more visible to the rest. It is in this historical context that, in both the poor and the rich worlds, deprivation, particularly of basic physical necessities, has come to be seen as more and more unacceptable. A further difficulty of the current context for African states is that some other parts of the world, notably South-East Asia, have rapidly expanded their productive capabilities in areas where Africa has a natural advantage, in some ways making it more difficult for African economies.

The second point is perhaps one which many will find difficult to accept, but which seems persuasive. The forces that determine historical change are overwhelmingly internal to societies. To revisit an earlier example, British, Japanese and Korean industrialisations, while similar in some ways, all took place in different contexts; but the major determinants of those processes, the reasons why they turned out the way they did, were the forces within those societies. Social, economic and political institutions and practices can only be forged from within; they cannot be foisted on people. Nowhere have choices about forms of social and political order, and about ways to make the transition from poverty to relative (if unequal) prosperity been made without mistakes, without disputes and disagreements, without temporary setbacks, all of which may, and often do, involve conflict. Such conflict can be handled in many different ways, but violent resolutions are often an inevitable part of historical change.

How might these considerations usefully shape relations between Africa and the West? Well: how does Britain deal with France? Or the United States deal with India? They do so in terms of respect for sovereignty, which means they do not interfere in each other's internal affairs and, for public purposes at least, they speak to each other in terms of respect. A glance at the news bulletins shows how seriously states take such matters. Of course these norms can be breached. States do attempt to manipulate other states; most major states almost certainly spy on each other's communications; occasionally they (respectfully) signal their disapproval of other states' policies. European states, for example, will not extradite to the United States people charged with offences that might attract a death sentence. But these exceptions prove the rule. They are marginal or clandestine. By far the largest part of relations between states consists of bargaining over their interests. This does not mean that states (like people) are always clear about what their interests are, nor does it mean that states (like people) do not exaggerate or dissimulate about their interests. But when France defends its film industry, the US subsidises its cotton farmers, or Britain protects the City of London, the motivations are not particularly puzzling.

So the first suggestion is that we should treat African states the same way we treat other states. We do not fund political parties in France, nor tell Germany how to run its economy, and we do not lecture Finland on its education system (lucky Finns!). Indeed, most Western countries specifically forbid external interference in their domestic politics. To treat other states as possessing sovereignty, and managing relationships with them in the framework of interests, is not just a self-interested calculation of advantage, but also a matter of respect. It is to treat them as one would wish to be treated oneself, as having aspirations but also a history and culture that determines who one is. When Africans struggled for independence, this is what they were demanding. There is no going back on that historic change openly, and we should not try to do so covertly, which is what the Western project has, for nearly thirty years, been trying to do.

It will of course be argued that respect for sovereignty and non-interference in domestic affairs as between, say, Britain and France, or Spain and Italy, works because those countries have so much in common. But this is to surreptitiously reintroduce notions like the 'standard of civilisation' – that some states are properly sovereign, and others are not. The fact is that sovereignty is only worth having if everyone has the same kind. African states have only been independent for sixty years, and are clearly in many ways still in the making. We should abandon assumptions that African states must eventually come to look like Western states. This may happen, and there are many forces trying to make it happen, but it may not. At present, many African states are not very 'state-like' according to the standard criteria. Many continue to experience large-scale conflict or political instability. State institutions are often non-existent or do not function. Ruling elites are often little more than tacit alliances between a number of groups. This is the familiar litany of 'state failure'. True, but it rather misses the point that in all sorts of ways forms of social and political order do work in Africa, and Africans may yet devise novel forms of politics that do not simply mimic developments elsewhere. On these grounds, as well as those of sovereignty, we should not interfere at all in the internal politics of African states. Much the same considerations apply to the fabric of African societies. We may find the ways in which African societies treat marriage or children or old people or animals strange, even repellent; but they are their ways. African societies are not uniform, and there is vigorous debate in Africa itself about all of these issues. Even if we find the idea of human rights appealing or compelling, a moment's thought shows that such rights are implemented in very different ways in different societies. For some, the Catholic Church, in its attitudes towards women and homosexuality, is in breach of human rights. But no Western state is planning to take on the Catholic Church. By what right do we demand of Africans more than we demand of ourselves?

WHAT ABOUT 'DEVELOPMENT'?

Realism shows that we should stop treating African states like children, but it does not prevent us from seeing that African peoples and governments may need certain kinds of support. Our ethical instincts tell us we should help where we can, where that help is likely to be effective, and where we can sustain it. Our common sense tells us that leaving large parts of the world impoverished and unstable is not good for anybody. Sociological realism tells us that there are no rulebooks or magic bullets that will always work. So how should we understand development? What grounds do we have for thinking it can be achieved? And how should we support it?

Many things have changed in Africa since independence; some for the better. Some countries (Botswana, Ghana, Gabon) are now classified as 'middle-income'. Some provide a degree of welfare and other services for their people. Many have sustained quite high rates of economic growth over quite long periods in the last decade. Some have used that period of economic growth to reduce their dependence on foreign aid and pay off much of their debt. But one thing has hardly changed: the economies of virtually all African countries remain very unproductive relative to their populations and potential, and they remain extremely dependent on the production and export of unprocessed primary goods, either minerals or crops.

Practically no African country has other African countries as its primary export market. Not one African country has a manufactured product in its top three exports. In some cases, countries have become more dependent on exports of raw materials than they were in the past. This dependence has several downsides. One is that natural resources are finite. Botswana, sub-Saharan Africa's success story, relies for 60% of its exports on diamonds, which are probably past their peak production. Ghana's oil is projected to last until 2030; Uganda's until 2040. And demand for raw materials can change relatively suddenly due to technological progress, for which African countries are ill-prepared (optic fibre for copper, solar energy for oil, etc.). Indeed, the prices of raw materials vary much more dramatically than those of manufactured goods, and over long periods their prices tend to decline relative to manufactured goods prices.

Beyond this dependence, many African countries have low domestic savings rates, domestic investment and agricultural productivity. With the partial exception of telecommunications, direct foreign investment in Africa is concentrated in minerals and mining. The social consequences of this economic situation are well known. Many Africans remain desperately poor, despite increasing growth rates; much of this growth generates very few jobs, so many African countries have high rates of disguised unemployment, especially among young men. Huge numbers of people scratch a living in the 'informal sector'. Because African economies are weak and societies often unstable, African elites stash enormous sums of money overseas. Many other problems are exacerbated by these economic difficulties.

These facts cast a rather harsh light on the recent optimism about Africa, all the heady talk about 'African Lions' and 'Africa leading the way'. For the simple fact is that since Africa exports predominantly raw materials, in situations where commodity markets are booming Africa will do well. And commodity markets have been booming in large part because of the extraordinary expansion of the Chinese and other East Asian economies, as they industrialise. But if those markets start to tumble, as from time to time they do, then Africa sinks. The most dramatic illustration of this is the recent collapse in oil prices, which has seen African 'giants' Nigeria and Angola, whose foreign trade and government revenue is almost wholly dependent on the export of crude oil, running to the IMF for financial support.

Looked at from this angle, the conventional responses to the 'problem of development' have missed the point. Development in Africa has been monopolised by an unholy alliance of charitable NGOs and international financial institutions. The first has lived off the idea that 'the problem' is poverty, the solution to which is limitless foreign aid. The second has championed Western mainstream economic wisdom, which has meant the imposition on Africa of 'sound' economic policies, also facilitated by huge amounts of aid. Some fifty years of these policies, in even the most optimistic assessments, have produced little change. In reality, 'the problem' is how to ensure that African economies become more productive and diverse so that they generate more employment. That is the real basis for economic security, the reduction of poverty, and a stable political order.

It seems unavoidable that this task must be approached from Africa's strength, which is its mineral wealth. It has vast oil reserves, and for a wide range of minerals it has half the world's known reserves. So African countries must learn how to do more with these resources than have someone else come and dig them out of the ground, take them away, and make things out of them. This is easy to say and difficult to do. The first difficulty is that the policies to be pursued cannot be simply derived from abstract principles. We get engineers, not physicists, to build planes. The most successful economy in modern times, both in terms of growth and poverty reduction, is China, which ignored virtually every element of the 'Washington Consensus' rulebook enjoined on Africa. The second difficulty is that each African country is different: some countries have more agricultural or tourism potential than others, some are landlocked, some have relatively highly educated populations, and so on. It is extremely unlikely that outsiders will ever have either the degree of local knowledge or legitimacy needed to successfully implement such production and diversification strategies.

There are still good reasons to hope that Africa can overcome its difficulties. The first is global economic trends. We noted earlier that the expansion of China and the South-East Asian countries had crowded out areas of economic activity where Africa might have had an advantage. That picture is now changing. As China and the other East Asian countries grow and transform their economies, their costs are rising, and the opportunities at the 'lower end' of the value chain become less attractive. Growing domestic demand is likely to shift manufacturing to the domestic market. Wages are also rising, leaving a gap for economies with lower labour costs.

There have been dramatic changes in the wider international economy. Huge reductions in global transport costs have meant that industrial processes once carried out by one firm in one country are increasingly split into different tasks carried out by different firms in different countries. The Apple iPhone is assembled in China, with major parts made in Korea, Japan and Germany, and smaller parts from a number of other countries. This way of manufacturing opens up possibilities for less technically advanced economies to attract some of the manufacturing activity for which they are more suited than their competitors. This is important because it is much easier to master parts of a production process than all its stages at once, and such processes provide opportunities to move on to more sophisticated technologies. Turning raw wood into sheets is easier than making furniture, but is also a step on the way to making furniture. A third effect of the fall in transport and communication costs has been to create a growing global market for trade in services, seasonal crops (fresh fruit, vegetables and flowers) and tourism. African countries have the potential to capture a significant proportion of these markets.

So while we cannot devise precise guidelines that apply to all situations, we can make some fruitful generalisations as to what is likely to help develop productive economies. Numerous commentators have drawn attention to a host of factors that have a bearing on enhancing Africa's economic diversification. Some have insisted on the importance of underlying factors – for example, 'human capital' – the educational level and skills of populations. They point to the fact that only 60% of Africa's 15- to 24-year-olds have completed primary school, and only about 20% have gone beyond lower secondary school. Others have drawn attention to the need to support enterprises. Peasant farmers need agricultural extension services, small-scale credit, and encouragement to experiment with new crops. Small businesses need credit and training in management. Almost everywhere, this requires state participation. This has led other analysts to point to the importance of institutions and the regulatory environment. States can foster business-supporting agencies like development banks and business incubators. They can set up research and development institutes. Even compared to other developing countries, African governments invest little in research and development. Yet other observers have stressed the importance of industrial policies to encourage production and exports. Governments can reduce the time and processes needed to set up a business, get permits or licensing. They can create export-promotion agencies and encourage cooperation between firms. The success of China's Export Processing Zones is frequently referred to as an example of such a policy.

These various explanations and policy implications are not of course incompatible, and they all almost certainly have a bearing on economic growth. Yet together they suffer from three significant drawbacks. First, in many cases it is not easy to determine the priorities and the effects of these policy areas. Is completing primary enrolment the priority? Should university education get more resources? Should technical subjects get priority? Second, they cover such a wide range of issues that pursuing them might diffuse effort and reinforce different donor agendas – reviving the bad tendencies that even the aid lobby concedes are a problem. Third, they would entail endless meddling in virtually every aspect of African societies which, I have argued, is neither morally justified nor politically effective.

There is, however, one sector of activity that does not suffer these drawbacks to the same extent, and is agreed on all sides to be a major priority. Indeed, we have already noted its significance for changes in the international economy. If it is not easy to say what makes economies more productive, it is perhaps easier to identify what no modern productive economy has been able to do without: communications infrastructure and electricity supply. The first of these is hardly controversial. Africa is the least integrated continent in the world. It has few navigable rivers and sixteen landlocked countries. Climates are often harsh, roads and bridges can deteriorate rapidly or even be washed away by flooding. Intra-continental trade is low at around 10–12%, and the continent's share of global exports is around 3%. Transport costs in Africa are some of the highest in the world; it often costs more to ship goods within Africa than it does from Africa to China. The railway system has changed little since colonial times; maintenance cultures are often haphazard or absent. In particular, rural Africa badly lacks communication networks of all kinds, even quite modest things like 'feeder roads', the benefits of which are well known. The Democratic Republic of Congo, a country four times the size of France, has fewer miles of paved road than Luxembourg. Only 30% of rural Africans live within a mile of an all-weather road. Roads carry about 75% of Africa's traffic, and about half of them are in poor condition. Most African ports are extremely inefficient by global standards.

The benefits of better infrastructure are fairly clear. Railways are the most efficient way of transporting bulk goods. Africa's rapid population growth is producing urbanisation, but much of this will be in medium-sized cities which will need non-motorised passenger transit systems. Roads make for easier access to services and better functioning markets, which raises output and helps to reduce poverty. Building them is labour intensive but relatively unskilled, and therefore provides (local) job opportunities. As transport costs are a high proportion of the prices of African products, more efficient ports will make African economies more competitive. Huge investment in the East African port of Mombasa has reduced the 'dwell times' (the time taken to unload and remove merchandise from the port) for ships to something like the global average, and it is here that the economy begins to look more competitive.

The other fundamental for modern economies is electricity supply. About 30% of the African population has access to electricity, which is very low even compared to other developing regions. In quite a number of countries that figure is under 20%. Boiling a kettle twice a day in the UK uses five times more electricity than a person in Mali uses on average in a whole year. The whole of sub-Saharan Africa produces less energy than Canada, and about half of that is generated by South Africa; excluding South Africa, sub-Saharan Africa produces less electricity than Spain. Even where firms and households are connected to a grid, there are constant interruptions to supply, sometimes lasting hours, even in South Africa. In Nigeria, most of the population are connected, but only 20% of those connections work more than half the time. Many individuals and firms keep generators, which is an extremely expensive way of maintaining electricity supply. Others use charcoal, candles and kerosene for lighting and cooking, which is both expensive for them and has environmental consequences which are bad for all of us. At the current rate of progress, some studies have suggested that it will be 2080 before all Africans have access to electricity.

The point is frequently made that while investment in transport infrastructure and electricity generation seem relatively uncontroversial preconditions for highly productive economies, they are not a magic wand. Africa's problems are not limited to physical road and rail links, but involve the management of border posts, the issue of 'dwell times' at ports, the structure of transport services and the trucking industry, the poor current performance of which contributes to considerable economic inefficiencies. Roads are targeted both by corrupt police and criminals, and bribes often constitute a large part of transport costs. Infrastructure projects are notorious for corruption and collusion through overpricing of materials, fake invoicing and transfer pricing, as well as a tendency to produce white elephants. Nearly fifty years ago, the Inga Dams in DRC were the centrepiece of a failed industrial development scheme. Poorly maintained for many years, the dams operated far below their capacity. They and a 1,770 km transmission line contributed heavily to the country's spiralling debt crisis. White elephants do not come much bigger than this. Nor have such episodes ceased. Nacala, in Mozambique, has a new airport, opened in 2014, built on the site of a former military facility, and costing $144 million. Its runway is 3,100 metres long, has a capacity of 500,000 passengers per year, and can take aircraft up to the size of a Boeing 747. But so far it has only one flight a day from Maputo (the capital), and no foreign airline has expressed any interest in flying there.*

Though acknowledging that infrastructure development, like anything else, has attendant difficulties, it remains central to putting Africa on the path to a more diversified economy, not only because of the immediate benefits it brings but also the spillover effects in a number of areas which, as noted earlier, have been widely identified as important to Africa's economic development. Infrastructure projects can have a significant impact on regional cooperation between African states on everything from railway gauges to power transmission standards, and that would help to translate vague aspirations into real progress. African governments and the African Union have acknowledged the importance of infrastructure, and done important preparatory work on a number of key transport corridors throughout the continent, aiming to connect African countries by road and rail, bringing about dramatic reductions in delivery times and considerable increases in capacity. Even without such projects in place, the countries of East Africa have made considerable progress in speeding up customs clearance and cargo

---

* That said, we should not imagine that such things only happen in poor countries. About a hundred miles south of Madrid is Ciudad Real Central airport, which cost a billion euros to build, can handle 10 million passengers a year, and closed after three years of operation.

handling. The countries of southern Africa have been developing a 'power pool' that enables them to share electricity and further develop the region's capacity. Other regions in Africa are pursuing the same model.

Beyond regional cooperation, infrastructure requires governments to learn the arts of regulation and maintenance. A major cause of road deterioration in Africa is the failure to enforce weight limits. Preventing breaches requires weighbridges and law enforcement. A substantial proportion of rail investment is now going into the rehabilitation and maintenance of the existing network. Infrastructure construction projects are also labour intensive, providing employment opportunities for a variety of skill levels. While some of that employment will be temporary, some can be used to train employees. Although built by a French construction firm, a new toll bridge in Abidjan, the capital of Côte d'Ivoire, which opened in 2014, employed and trained 1,400 Ivorians. Most of the materials used in its construction were Ivorian, except for some specialised items, as the contract specified maximum use of local resources. The consortium administering the thirty-year contract to operate the bridge has 160 employees, almost all of whom are local. Infrastructure projects can stimulate demand for goods (cement, basic chemicals, clothing) that can be produced locally and, with the right policies in place, generate business for local enterprises. Infrastructure projects can be financed and managed in a variety of ways which would stimulate Africa's capital markets and financial institutions generally.

A NEW POLITICAL BARGAIN

So it seems clear that where Africa most needs support in order to become more productive is in the areas of infrastructure-building, renewal and maintenance. Something of a new consensus is emerging on these issues. The Sustainable Development Goals, adopted by the UN in September 2015, talk about 'sustained economic growth' and 'inclusive and sustainable industrialisation'. African states have adopted a Programme for Infrastructure Development (PIDA). About 20% of World Bank lending is now going towards transport projects, and in 2014 it launched a Global Infrastructure Fund. Since 2007, the EU has financed an Africa Infrastructure Trust Fund. Within this new emphasis on infrastructure, a number of recent initiatives have focused on energy. The United Nations launched its global Sustainable Energy for All initiative in 2012 to pull 1 billion people out of energy poverty, 500 million of them in Africa. In June 2013, US President Obama launched Power Africa, a partnership among the US government, African governments, bilateral and multilateral development partners, and the private sector to double access to electricity in sub-Saharan Africa, adding 300,000 megawatts and 60 million connections to Africa by 2030. The African Development Bank has launched a New Deal for Energy in Africa, and the British government is promoting an Energy Africa campaign, focusing on renewable energy for rural populations living off the grid. Along with this official encouragement, there have been efforts to recruit the private sector into the creation of infrastructure. A number of groupings, such as the Continental Business Network and the Africa50 Infrastructure Fund, have been formed to promote public–private dialogue and funding.

This is all very encouraging, and it would be churlish to dismiss what seem to be the beginnings of a genuine shift in policy, along with the (quiet) abandonment of a great deal of dogmatism. But we have, after all, been here before. Asserting that 'an adequate supply of power, communications and transportation facilities is a precondition for the…industrialisation and diversification of the underdeveloped countries' sounds very modern. It is in fact taken from the World Bank's annual report of 1951. The Organisation of African Unity prepared a railways 'master plan' in 1979. The Trans-African Highway was floated in 1971. It is easy to make declarations, devise plans and proposals, and to raise external finance for them. Turning those declarations and proposals into reality is more difficult.

The planning and technical problems of infrastructure development are well understood; it is the political and ideological difficulties that need to be overcome. Programmes wither, political energies dissipate, and the siren songs of various lobbies are only temporarily hushed. What is needed is a new more honest political bargain between the West and Africa. This bargain should include accepting the sovereignty of African states in the full sense, and on the same terms, as we accept the sovereignty of other states. We should forgo virtue signalling and moral posturing. We should abandon the calls for African elites to be moral saints without interests, but should rather seek to harness those interests to a more coherent economic project. The countries of South-East Asia, or anywhere else for that matter, did not develop because their elites abandoned self-interest or became ascetics. Curtailing corruption will not come from external preaching, but from African enterprises demanding a minimum level of state competence and efficiency. We should operate no punitive regimes, inducements or conditionalities that single out African states for special treatment, or insist they pursue particular policies.

Once normal relations with African states are restored, we should acknowledge that almost all sub-Saharan African states face deep-rooted economic difficulties, and there is a strong case for assisting them to overcome those difficulties. That assistance should be provided on the basis of common objectives and interests where possible, and solidarity where there is a plausible need. China has shown the way here, offering support for infrastructure in exchange for guarantees of long-term supply of raw materials. There is no reason why richer countries should not pursue their interests provided African countries can also pursue theirs. This would be politically healthy on all sides. It would help to make a much more plausible case for support for the economic transformation of Africa to domestic audiences in the West, rather than endlessly stressing poverty and deprivation.

It is not possible here to elaborate the detailed implications of such a political clearing of the decks, but it would at least make possible a new development bargain. It would signal the end of aid as perpetual life support. It would make clear that while no specific policy conditions should be imposed, African governments are responsible for their countries' development. Doubtless outside advice and expertise would have an important role to play, but project proposals would have to come from African governments, be coherent with their own national policies, and be driven forward by them. Support would be prioritised towards governments and regional organisations showing themselves able to identify needs, propose plans, oversee their implementation and subsequently maintain the results. Within such a framework, Western support would be shifted into a highly targeted commitment to the development of infrastructure, with a relentless focus on projects having demonstrably positive effects on production, productivity and employment.

Such a shift will not solve all problems. It will not abolish war or conflict or poverty. It will not bring about a heaven on (African) earth. But the energy of 1 billion people in sub-Saharan Africa is currently constrained by the absence of relatively simple technologies that most of the rest of the world takes for granted. We cannot tell Africans how to live, but we can help to remove those constraints. Let us help not hector. We can do no more, but we should surely do no less.

READING GUIDES

CHAPTER 1: GUILT

It is curious that the further in time we get away from imperialism and colonialism the more controversial they become. For a generally sympathetic account of British colonialism, see N. Ferguson, *Empire: How Britain Made the Modern World* (London: Penguin, 2004). For a deeply hostile one, see J. Newsinger, *The Blood Never Dried* (London: Bookmarks, 2013). Perhaps the most balanced recent account is J. Darwin, *Unfinished Empire: The Global Expansion of Britain* (London: Penguin, 2013). Much shorter is A. Jackson, *The British Empire: A Very Short Introduction* (Oxford: Oxford University Press, 2013).

If the literature on empire is controversial, that on race is even more heated. Until very recently both popular and scholarly writing were entirely dominated by the notion that race was a malicious European invention (a curious exception to complaints about 'eurocentrism'!) unknown in the rest of the world. It is not hard to see the political advantages of this notion, but it has been undermined by research on China and Japan. For the evidence, see F. Dikötter, 'The racialization of the globe: an interactive interpretation', *Ethnic and Racial Studies*, 31(8),

2008, pp. 1478–96. For a more general discussion, see A. Bonnett, 'Multiple racializations in a multiply modern world', *Ethnic and Racial Studies* (Leiden, 2017), pp. 1–18. There has been little work on Africa around this theme, but one example would be J. Brennan, *Taifa: Making Nation and Race in Urban Tanzania* (Athens, OH: Ohio University Press, 2012). Though it leans to the orthodox view, there is a fair discussion of the issue of Western philosophy and race at http://www.thecritique.com/articles/the-roots-of-modern-racism/. The best account of Locke and slavery is probably J. Farr, 'Locke, natural law, and new world slavery', *Political Theory*, 36(4), 2008, pp. 495–522.

The participation of Africans in the slave trade is hardly news for historians. The pioneer work here was J. Thornton, *Africa and Africans in the Making of the Atlantic World, 1400–1800* (Cambridge: Cambridge University Press, 1998), but the point is increasingly being acknowledged in popular discussion, including in Africa itself. It has even been the subject of a film, *Adanggaman*, by the Ivorian director Roger M'Bala. On other slave trades, see R. Segal, *Islam's Black Slaves: The Other Black Diaspora* (New York: Macmillan, 2002), and R.C. Davis, *Christian Slaves, Muslim Masters: White Slavery in the Mediterranean, the Barbary Coast and Italy, 1500–1800* (Basingstoke: Palgrave Macmillan, 2003). On the 'African scramble for Africa' see, for example, B.J. Peterson, 'History, memory and the legacy of Samori in southern Mali, *c.* 1880–1898', *Journal of African History*, 49(2), 2008, pp. 261–79. On fresh looks at African nationalism, see J.-B. Gewald, M. Hinfelaar and G. Macola (eds), *Living the End of Empire: Politics and Society in Late Colonial Zambia* (Brill Academic Publishers, 2011).

CHAPTER 2: $22,000 FOR EIGHTEEN CUPS OF TEA

The best background book is D. Williams, *International Development and Global Politics: History, Theory and Practice*

(Abingdon: Routledge, 2011). D.H. Lumsdaine, *Moral Vision in International Politics: The Foreign Aid Regime 1949–1989* (Princeton: Princeton University Press, 1993) stresses the moral aspects of aid. G. Van Bilzen, *The Development of Aid* (Newcastle upon Tyne: Cambridge Scholars Publishing, 2015) is an encyclopaedic survey of the whole period since the Second World War. For the expensive cups of tea (and much else besides) see S. Berkman, *The World Bank and the Gods of Lending* (Sterling, VA: Kumarian Press, 2008). O. Therkildsen, *Watering White Elephants? Lessons from Donor Funded Planning and Implementation of Rural Water Supplies in Tanzania* (Uppsala: Scandinavian Institute of African Studies, 1988) illustrates many of the points made in this chapter.

A short but interesting set of reflections on the earlier period of aid is N. Birdsall, 'Seven deadly sins: reflections on donor failings', Working Paper Number 50 (Washington: Centre for Global Development, 2004) (available online). For an impressionistic account of elite wealth, see M. Wrong, 'When the money goes West', *New Statesman*, 14 March 2005. There is a more technical short account of elite wealth in L. Ndikumana and J.K. Boyce, 'Rich presidents of poor nations: capital flight from resource-rich countries in Africa', *ACAS Bulletin*, 87, 2012, pp. 2–7. On taxation, see M. Moore, 'Death without taxes: democracy, state capacity, and aid dependence in the fourth world', in *The Democratic Developmental State: Politics and Institutional Design*, ed. M. Robinson and G. White (Oxford: Oxford University Press, 1998). For a more sceptical view, but also a useful discussion of taxation and state-building issues, see O. Therkildsen, 'Understanding taxation in poor African countries: a critical review of selected perspectives', *Forum for Development Studies*, 28(1), 2001, pp. 99–123.

CHAPTER 3: TURNING A BLIND EYE

There are a number of good books on post-independence African politics. More journalistic, but full of information is M. Meredith, *The State of Africa* (London: Simon & Schuster, 2006). More academic and wide-ranging is P. Nugent, *Africa Since Independence* (Basingstoke: Palgrave Macmillan, 2004). J. Herbst, *States and Power in Africa: Comparative Lessons in Authority and Control* (Princeton: Princeton University Press, 2014) has a very useful focus on state consolidation.

On the dangers of African politics, see J.A. Wiseman, 'Leadership and personal danger in African politics', *Journal of Modern African Studies*, 31(4), 1993, pp. 657–60, and for patterns of violence, S. Straus, 'Wars do end! Changing patterns of political violence in sub-Saharan Africa', *African Affairs*, 111(443), 2012, pp. 179–201. On Burundi, R. Lemarchand and D. Martin, *Selective Genocide in Burundi* (London: Minority Rights Group, 1974) was the first serious reporting of the 1972 massacres. Extracts from this are in T. Young (ed.), *Readings in the International Relations of Africa* (Bloomington, IN: Indiana University Press, 2016). For aspects of liberation movements that were virtually taboo until recently, see P. Trewhela, *Inside Quatro: Uncovering the Exile History of the ANC and SWAPO* (Johannesburg: Jacana Media, 2009).

For the view that Africa's problems were due to external forces, see G. Arrighi, 'The African crisis', *New Left Review*, 15, May/June 2002, pp. 5–36. The extremely useful journal *Review of African Political Economy* retains a rather nostalgic tendency in this direction. Africa's economic decline in the 1990s is discussed from a variety of angles in T.M. Callaghy and J. Ravenhill (eds), *Hemmed In: Responses to Africa's Economic Decline* (New York: Columbia University Press, 1993).

On the connections between politics and development it is best to look at particular situations. K. Skinner, 'Who knew the minds of the people? Specialist knowledge and developmentalist authoritarianism in postcolonial Ghana', *Journal of Imperial and Commonwealth History*, 39(2), 2011, pp. 297–323 and L. Schneider, 'Colonial legacies and postcolonial authoritarianism in Tanzania: connects and disconnects', *African Studies Review*, 49(1), 2006, pp. 93–118 suggest that many African states did take development seriously. R. Tangri and A.M. Mwenda, *The Politics of Elite Corruption in Africa: Uganda in Comparative African Perspective* (Abingdon: Routledge, 2013) tells the other side of the story. There is a nice example of the connections with aid in R.C. Briggs, 'Aiding and abetting: project aid and ethnic politics in Kenya', *World Development*, 64, 2014, pp. 194–205.

CHAPTER 4: THE PUNITIVE TURN

The idea of 'neopatrimonialism' has spawned an enormous academic and policy literature. The best introduction to it is still P. Chabal and J.-P. Daloz, *Africa Works: Disorder as Political Instrument* (Oxford: James Currey, 1999). Reaction to it has been suitably ferocious, even venomous. Overplaying its hand at times, and occasionally shrill, the best critique is T. Mkandawire, 'Neopatrimonialism and the political economy of economic performance in Africa: critical reflections', *World Politics*, 67(3), 2015, pp. 563–612, which reveals the main weaknesses of the idea. T. Kelsall, 'Neo-patrimonialism, rent-seeking and development: going with the grain?', *New Political Economy*, 17(5), 2012, pp. 677–82 suggests why, weaknesses notwithstanding, it is still a useful idea.

For the 'standard of civilisation', B. Bowden, 'In the name of progress and peace: the "standard of civilization" and the universalizing project', *Alternatives*, 29(1), 2004, pp. 43–68 provides lots of historical background, while M. Mazower, 'An international civilisation? Empire, internationalism and the crisis of the mid-twentieth century', *International Affairs*, 82(3), 2006, pp. 553–66 looks at the more recent period.

A useful general work on conflict in Africa is P.D. Williams, *War and Conflict in Africa* (Cambridge: Polity, 2011). On Mozambique see M. Hall and T. Young, *Confronting Leviathan: Mozambique since Independence* (London: Hurst & Co., 1997). For the view that sees invading other people's countries as progress see A.J. Bellamy and P.D. Williams, 'The new politics of protection? Côte d'Ivoire, Libya and the responsibility to protect', *International Affairs*, 87(4), 2011, pp. 825–50. For more plausible accounts, see A.J. Kuperman, 'A model humanitarian intervention? Reassessing NATO's Libya campaign', *International Security*, 38(1), 2013, pp. 105–36 and H. Roberts, 'Who said Gaddafi had to go?', *London Review of Books*, 17 November 2011. For Côte d'Ivoire, see A. Mehler, 'From "protecting civilians" to "for the sake of democracy" (and back again): justifying intervention in Côte d'Ivoire', *African Security*, 5(3–4), 2012, pp. 199–216. The best book on Côte d'Ivoire is M. McGovern, *Making War in Côte d'Ivoire* (London: Hurst & Co., 2011).

CHAPTER 5: IMPOSING RULES

The Bretton Woods Institutions attract considerable hostility. A short and reasonably fair-minded summary of the World Bank is in J.M.M. Pereira, 'Recycling and expansion: an analysis of the World Bank agenda (1989–2014)', *Third World Quarterly*, 37(5), 2016, pp. 818–39. Much more critical is J. Pincus and J. Winters (eds), *Reinventing the World Bank* (Ithaca, NY: Cornell University Press, 2002). More mainstream, and covering both institutions, is N. Woods, *The Globalizers: The IMF, the World Bank and Their Borrowers* (Ithaca, NY: Cornell University Press, 2006).

J. Pender, 'From "structural adjustment" to "comprehensive development framework": conditionality transformed?', *Third*

World Quarterly, 22(3), 2001, pp. 397–411 describes the shift away from structural adjustment. For good critical guides to various conditionalities, see J. Gould (ed.), *The New Conditionality: The Politics of Poverty Reduction Strategies* (London: Zed Books, 2005) and A. Fraser, 'Poverty reduction strategy papers: now who calls the shots?', *Review of African Political Economy*, 32(104–5), 2005, pp. 317–40. For a specific case, see L. Whitfield, 'The state elite, PRSPs and policy implementation in aid-dependent Ghana', *Third World Quarterly*, 31(5), 2010, pp. 721–37. R. Youngs, 'European approaches to democracy assistance: learning the right lessons?', *Third World Quarterly*, 24(1), 2003, pp. 127–38 covers the earlier period of political conditionalities. N. Molenaers, S. Dellepiane and J. Faust, 'Political conditionality and foreign aid', *World Development*, 75, 2015, pp. 2–12 brings the story up to date.

Virtually all the writing about sanctions consists of debates about how to 'improve' them. G.M. Khadiagala, 'Global and regional mechanisms for governing the resource curse in Africa', *Politikon: South African Journal of Political Studies*, 42(1), 2015, pp. 23–43 covers the mainstream perspectives. J.A. Grant, 'Commonwealth cousins combating conflict diamonds: an examination of South African and Canadian contributions to the Kimberley Process', *Commonwealth & Comparative Politics*, 51(2), 2013, pp. 210–33, describes the Kimberley process. For sanctions aimed at individuals, see P. Wallensteen and H. Grusell, 'Targeting the right targets? The UN use of individual sanctions', *Global Governance*, 18, 2012, pp. 207–30.

CHAPTER 6: CHANGING CONDUCT

The book that has shaped much of my approach in this chapter is D. Williams, *The World Bank and Social Transformation in International Politics* (Abingdon: Routledge, 2008). A shorter sceptical discussion of governance is M. Andrews, 'The good governance agenda: beyond indicators without theory', *Oxford Development Studies*, 36(4), 2008, pp. 379–407. V. Chhotray and D. Hulme, 'Contrasting visions for aid and governance in the 21st century: the White House Millennium Challenge Account and DFID's drivers of change', *World Development*, 37(1), 2009, pp. 36–49 provides more details and shows how donors can differ on these matters.

G. Crawford and G. Lynch (eds), *Democratization in Africa: Challenges and Prospects* (Abingdon: Routledge, 2012) and D. Resnick and N. van de Walle (eds), *Democratic Trajectories in Africa: Unravelling the Impact of Foreign Aid* (Oxford: Oxford University Press, 2013) both contain numerous case studies. For the scale of Western involvement, see E. Gyimah-Boadi and T. Yakah, 'Ghana: the limits of external democracy assistance', Working Paper No. 2012/40 (Helsinki: United Nations University, April 2012).

J. Erk, 'Federalism and decentralization in sub-Saharan Africa: five patterns of evolution', *Regional & Federal Studies*, 24(5), 2014, pp. 535–52 is a brief introduction to issues of decentralisation. D. Resnick, 'Urban governance and service delivery in African cities: the role of politics and policies', *Development Policy Review*, 32(S1), 2014, pp. s3–s17 looks at some of the evidence. For a detailed case see C.D. Gore and N.K. Muwanga, 'Decentralization is dead, long live decentralization! Capital city reform and political rights in Kampala, Uganda', *International Journal of Urban and Regional Research*, 38(6), 2014, pp. 2201–16.

The approach to civil society in this chapter derives from D. Williams and T. Young, 'Civil society and the liberal project in Ghana and Sierra Leone', *Journal of Intervention and Statebuilding*, 6(1), 2012, pp. 7–22, which also briefly explains the theoretical background to the concept.

M. Mazower, 'The strange triumph of human rights, 1933–1950', *The Historical Journal*, 47(2), 2004, pp. 379–98 is good background for the politics of human rights. There is more detail, as well as case studies, in S.-L. Hoffmann (ed.), *Human Rights in the Twentieth Century* (Cambridge: Cambridge University Press, 2011), which has chapters on Chile and human rights and African nationalism. S. Harris-Short, 'International human rights law: imperialist, inept and ineffective? Cultural relativism and the UN Convention on the Rights of the Child', *Human Rights Quarterly*, 25, 2003, pp. 130–81 is a fair-minded discussion of the difficulties of squaring much African cultural practice with Western notions of human rights.

CHAPTER 7: A FAILED PROJECT

The aid debate never stops. The two big critics are W. Easterly, *The White Man's Burden: Why the West's Efforts to Aid the Rest Have Done So Much Ill and So Little Good* (Oxford: Oxford University Press, 2007) and D. Moyo, *Dead Aid: Why Aid is Not Working and How There is Another Way for Africa* (London: Penguin, 2010). A short fair-minded account is S.W. Hook and J.G. Rumsey, 'The development aid regime at fifty: policy challenges inside and out', *International Studies Perspectives*, 17(1), 2016, pp. 55–74. Sympathetic, but critical and accessible, is J. Glennie, *The Trouble with Aid* (London: Zed Books, 2008). The same author has a go at translating economists' jargon for the rest of us in J. Glennie and A. Sumner, 'The $138.5 billion question: when does foreign aid work (and when doesn't it)?', CGD Policy Paper 49 (Washington, DC: Center for Global Development, 2014). There is a judicious summary of the broader issues in L. Ndikumana and L. Pickbourn, 'The future of aid effectiveness in sub-Saharan Africa – a research agenda', Global Development Network's Paper Series (see www.gdn.int/african-voicesonaid).

For the mainstream orthodoxy on humanitarian intervention,

see T.G. Weiss, *Humanitarian Intervention: Ideas in Action* (Cambridge: Polity, 2016). For various reasons to be sceptical, see N. Narang, 'Assisting uncertainty: how humanitarian aid can inadvertently prolong civil war', *International Studies Quarterly*, 2014, pp. 1–12, and J. Fisher and D.M. Anderson, 'Authoritarianism and the securitization of development in Africa', *International Affairs*, 91(1), 2015, pp. 131–51. For cases and detail, see S. Autesserre, 'The responsibility to protect in Congo: the failure of grassroots prevention', *International Peacekeeping*, 23(1), 2016, pp. 29–51 and A. Branch, 'Against humanitarian impunity: rethinking responsibility for displacement and disaster in Northern Uganda', *Journal of Intervention and Statebuilding*, 2(2), 2008, pp. 151–73.

C. Gegout, 'The International Criminal Court: limits, potential and conditions for the promotion of justice and peace', *Third World Quarterly*, 34(5), 2013, pp. 800–18 provides a mainstream view, generally positive, about the Court. A. Branch, 'Uganda's civil war and the politics of ICC intervention', *Ethics & International Affairs*, 21(2), 2007, pp. 179–98 suggests reasons to be sceptical. For the Sudan, see A. de Waal, 'When kleptocracy becomes insolvent: brute causes of the civil war in South Sudan', *African Affairs*, 113(452), 2014, pp. 347–69.

For the Botswana story, see J.S. Solway, 'Human rights and NGO "wrongs": conflict diamonds, culture wars and the "Bushman question"', *Africa*, 79(3), 2009, pp. 321–46, and S. Saugestad, 'Impact of international mechanisms on indigenous rights in Botswana', *International Journal of Human Rights*, 15(1), 2011, pp. 37–61.

CHAPTER 8: CHANGING DIRECTION

For peace-keeping, see M. Brosig, 'Rentier peacekeeping in neo-patrimonial systems: the examples of Burundi and Kenya', *Contemporary Security Policy*, 38(1), 2017, pp. 109–28. For the

Kenya story, see M. Wrong, *It's Our Turn to Eat: The Story of a Kenyan Whistleblower* (London: Fourth Estate, 2010). For corruption issues more generally, see T. Søreide and A. Williams (eds), *Corruption, Grabbing and Development: Real World Challenges* (Cheltenham: Edward Elgar, 2013). For a critical account of NGOs, even if from within the fold, see N. Banks with D. Hulme, 'The role of NGOs and civil society in development and poverty reduction', Brooks World Poverty Institute Working Paper No. 171 (Brooks World Poverty Institute, University of Manchester, 2012).

For a good challenge to current complacency about Africa's economic progress, see I. Taylor, 'Dependency redux: why Africa is not rising', *Review of African Political Economy*, 43(147), 2016, pp. 8–25. For thinking about industrialisation, see M. Morris and J. Fessehaie, 'The industrialisation challenge for Africa: towards a commodities based industrialisation path', *Journal of African Trade*, 1(1), 2014, pp. 25–36 and J. Page, 'Can Africa industrialise?', *Journal of African Economies*, 21, AERC Supplement 2, 2012, pp. ii86–ii125. For detailed case studies, including some comparison with Asia, see C. Newman, J. Page, J. Rand et al. (eds), *Manufacturing Transformation: Comparative Studies of Industrial Development in Africa and Emerging Asia* (Oxford: Oxford University Press, 2016).

On infrastructure for the plans, see F.N. Ikome and R.T. Lisinge, 'The political economy of infrastructure development in Africa: an assessment of the NEPAD Presidential Infrastructure Champion Initiative (PICI)', *Canadian Journal of African Studies*, 50(2), 2016, pp. 255–77, and for the current situation, T. Corrigan, 'Rethinking infrastructure in Africa: a governance approach', Occasional Paper 252 (Johannesburg: South African Institute of International Affairs, 2017). For electricity specifically, see A. Scott, 'Building electricity supplies in Africa for growth and universal access', background paper for *Power, People, Planet: Seizing Africa's energy and climate opportunities* (London and

Washington, DC: New Climate Economy, 2015), available at http://newclimateeconomy.report/misc/working-papers.

For the complexities of infrastructure projects, as well as an interesting study of China–Africa relations, see U. Wissenbach and Y. Wang, 'African politics meets Chinese engineers: the Chinese-built Standard Gauge Railway Project in Kenya and East Africa', Working Paper No. 2017/13 (Washington, DC: China*Africa Research Initiative, School of Advanced International Studies, Johns Hopkins University, 2017), available at www.sais-cari.org/publications.

ACKNOWLEDGEMENTS

It is frequently remarked that any book, though usually credited to a named author, is in fact the result of various forms of institutional and social support. This book is no exception. I am grateful to the Politics Department at the School of Oriental and African Studies for allowing me a sabbatical term in which to finish it, and the colleagues who generously covered for me during my absence. I am also grateful to my family for their forbearance during its writing, as well as the occasional vigorous dining-table discussions that made me think and helped me clarify arguments. Three friends, Peter Brett, David Williams and Bala Liman looked over the text, saved me from errors, posed questions and provided encouragement. Lastly, I would like to acknowledge the role of Alex Christofi and his colleagues at Oneworld. Alex did his very best to make the text as engaging and readable as possible, though I must take responsibility for its final form. I am especially thankful that, in the end, he came to accept my preferred title for the book which, I think, most clearly registers its key point.

INDEX